T0295687

The Self-Made Program Leader

Taking Charge in Matrix Organizations

Best Practices and Advances
in Program Management Series

Series Editor
Ginger Levin

The Self-Made Program Leader

Taking Charge in Matrix Organizations

Steve Tkalcevich

CRC Press
Taylor & Francis Group
Boca Raton   London   New York

CRC Press is an imprint of the
Taylor & Francis Group, an **informa** business
AN AUERBACH BOOK

CRC Press
Taylor & Francis Group
6000 Broken Sound Parkway NW, Suite 300
Boca Raton, FL 33487-2742

Printed on acid-free paper
Version Date: 20150616

International Standard Book Number-13: 978-1-4822-3313-1 (Hardback)

Visit the Taylor & Francis Web site at
http://www.taylorandfrancis.com

and the CRC Press Web site at
http://www.crcpress.com

Contents

Preface

This book was written to discuss working in matrix environments for project, program, and portfolio managers and to provide tactics to succeed. The matrix structure is becoming ever more popular, but there is not much evidence on how to operate successfully in a matrix. How does one manage oneself and lead others? This book takes a unique approach to understanding the matrix structure and tactics to succeed. Without a plan for success, leaders are left to operate in ways that may be less than efficient and ideal for their situation. This book began as a survey of 55 project, program, and portfolio managers who were asked 13 strategic questions. These questions are themes that are discussed throughout the book. The idea for this book came from my dissertation for my master of business administration degree with the University of Liverpool in 2012–2013. I was looking at novel ways to reduce employee turnover and increase workplace commitment for leaders.

Acknowledgments

I have been told that it is not the goal, but the journey that matters. Taking the time to acknowledge the smaller things people do for you in life and your career. Those are the things that you will remember and cherish in your later years. This book is a result of others taking the time to show me the right way to perform a task and help others as a result. I would like to thank my family for their guidance and all the mentors I had along the way—you all mean so much to me. A special thanks goes to the leaders who participated in the survey for this book's content, and the series editor, Dr. Ginger Levin.

Author

Steve Tkalcevich earned an MBA specializing in leadership from the University of Liverpool; he has held the PMP® designation from the Project Management Institute (PMI) since 2006, a master certificate in six sigma from Villanova University, and a diploma in microcomputer management from Humber College in Toronto, Canada.

Tkalcevich has worked in the information technology sector since 2000. For the last several years he has worked for various web software development firms in project management roles. Prior to working in project management, Tkalcevich worked in information technology management for a leading wholesale firm in Canada, as a technical support supervisor for an Internet service provider and in information technology consulting, where he started his career. Volunteering has been an important part of Tkalcevich's growth in his career with the PMI and other organizations.

Meeting the needs of his peers and clients has always been a key achievement for Tkalcevich. He learned early the value of successful relationships and how to maintain and grow them into something special.

Introduction

Ask yourself: Can you be an effective leader if you do not have the formal authority that is rooted in the organizational hierarchy? This question needs to be understood, and many others surrounding this topic will be studied in this book. It does not matter if you are beginning your first role as a project, program, or portfolio manager or if you are in the middle of a complex initiative, you need to determine how to maneuver in this territory. Working in a matrix organizational structure brings new challenges and likewise new opportunities for those who can capitalize and influence effectively. In roles where you have formal authority over your team, you cannot directly transfer the same approach into a matrix structure. In this book, I will show you proven strategies and behaviors that will let you deliver your projects, programs, and portfolios within their desired objectives and maintain mutually beneficial relationships both internally and externally.

Matrix structures come in various forms, as depicted in Table I.1, which shows the influence of organizational structures on projects. There are three variational (weak, balanced, and strong) structures in which a project, program, or portfolio manager can operate. Each has its own unique characteristics and challenges. Arguably, one style may be easier to maneuver in than others depending on one's personality when managing work, but they all have challenges that will need to be faced. The most challenging is the weak matrix for the leader

Table I.1   Influence on Organizational Structures on Projects

ORGANIZATION STRUCTURE PROJECT CHARACTERISTICS	FUNCTIONAL	WEAK MATRIX	BALANCED MATRIX	STRONG MATRIX	PROJECTIZED
Project manager's authority	Little or none	Low	Low to moderate	Moderate to high	High to almost total
Resource availability	Little or none	Low	Low to moderate	Moderate to high	High to almost total
Who manages the project budget	Functional manager	Functional manager	Mixed	Project manager	Project manager
Project manager's role	Part-time	Part-time	Full-time	Full-time	Full-time
Project management administrative staff	Part-time	Part-time	Part-time	Full-time	Full-time

Source: *A Guide to the Project Management Body of Knowledge* (PMBOK® guide, 5th edn.), Project Management Institute, Newtown Square, PA, 2013, p. 22. With permission.

where the functional manager has more authority over the team but the project, program, or portfolio manager still needs to achieve his or her deliverables.

Topping the list of challenges common to each variation are power struggles with functional mangers and the project, program, or portfolio manager; confusion with team members as to which direction to take when given two distinctly different decisions by managers and the leader; and not to mention an abundant amount of seemingly pointless meetings with all members not present at all times.

Matrix structures are not new to organizations, and have existed for decades. What this book does is provide a new approach to succeed in this structure, as what may have worked in other types cannot always be transferred to the matrix and achieve reasonable success by the project, program, or portfolio manager.

What you will get from this book is insight into the minds of a group of 55 project, program, and portfolio managers who work in a matrix environment, either currently or in past roles, who have been surveyed. Thirty percent of the participants surveyed have between 10 and 20-plus years of experience, while some were just beginning their careers in project, program, or portfolio management. These perspectives formulated the direction of the book and provided insight as to how these individuals lead others in a matrix environment. Some of them were unsuccessful at times, and this book will seek to understand why and learn from those who were successful. A total of 13 strategic questions were asked among the group that covered their respective roles as a project, program, or portfolio manager in a matrix environment. Insights into the answers of these questions are documented throughout the book. The results of the survey in its entirety can be found in the appendix of this book.

Understanding how the project, program, and portfolio manager fits within the matrix structure can sometimes cause confusion. It is important for this key point to be fully understood, as the book discusses many challenges this scenario brings to the leader. There are advantages of having a matrix structure at your company. One of them is that this practice makes good business sense, and shared resources are being used by multiple project, program, or portfolio managers who are being managed by a functional manager who oversees the administrative human resource responsibilities. Better utilization of human capital can be achieved by having a common pool of resources to use.

This book will not go into particulars on how to implement a matrix structure, but instead will focus on how to maneuver within them successfully. You will also learn the necessary behaviors that you need to demonstrate when interacting with others. Those who are new to this organizational structure or who have been working in it for multiple years will benefit equally from this book. The goal is to show a clear path for project, program, and portfolio managers to lead others within a matrix environment regardless of the industry or complexity. However, what is required on your part is the desire to improve, learn, and grow as a professional. Having periods of self-reflection of your leadership style and effectiveness is the way you will improve as a leader. Having a peer, mentor, a small group of professionals, or another individual whom you trust along the journey to discuss your progress will keep you heading in the right direction by providing you with feedback. These are the cornerstones of the principles the book will communicate.

When you join a professional organization, such as the PMI, you have the opportunity to participate in online communities or to join a local PMI chapter in your area. These groups provide learning resources, networking opportunities, volunteer roles, and the ability to have your questions answered, which facilitates knowledge sharing and collaboration. These opportunities will be discussed to show how they can increase your ability to have influence in your job, which you will find is a key aspect of those leaders who work in a matrix environment.

Influence has been mentioned several times already, but we have not gone into why it is desirable and important to your role. When you are able to influence your followers, you are able to meet their needs. Once needs are met, cooperation is much more likely. It should be understood that certain leadership styles, such as the authoritarian type of leader, will not be effective in a matrix structure. In fact, this approach can cause a great deal of damage and hostility within the team, as well as damage to the company's reputation. The "I lead, you follow" model is not appropriate to use in this situation. This book will discuss how to better position your leadership style to get maximum benefits. If you are coming from a position in which you had formal authority over your team, you will benefit particularly from this topic.

Influence is not the only skill that is required to be learned by the leader in a matrix structure. Understanding reciprocity, in that one good deed deserves another, and how to make the most out of a topic called *organizational currency* are some of the most useful tools that you can use in a matrix environment. These topics may be new to you, but they have a definitive place in your role in the organization. You may be practicing these techniques already and not even know it. These subjects will be discussed in detail, and you will see why they play such an important part in the success of your role as a project, program, or portfolio manager. Remember, without formal authority of your team, your leadership style needs to be adjusted accordingly; what was used in the past with having formal authority will not be successful for you right now.

It may be easier to provide several examples in your organizational life for which influence will play an essential part. This is not meant to be an extensive, inclusive list representative of a leader's role in the organization.

- Within your team, you find that the responsibilities are not evenly spread among the group, despite your appeals to the team to contribute more frequently and with greater effort.

- You are working with a specialist who does not always take your suggestions into consideration when needed, and it is negatively affecting your desired outcomes on your projects, programs, or portfolio. You have tried to remedy it, but to no avail—the situation remains the same.
- Your manager is frequently dealing with a "crisis," and you are not getting the time you need from this person when you need it. As a result your projects, programs, or portfolio is suffering the consequences. Even though you try to allocate time with your manager, you are not getting what is needed.
- You require the cooperation and commitment of someone from another department or organization for your project, programs, or portfolio. You have tried several methods and none seems to work on a regular basis.

These examples provide just some of the challenges that a project, program, or portfolio manager may encounter while working in a matrix structure. By understanding the organizational structure in any situation, you will greatly increase the level of success that you can have influencing others. To understand the situation you first need to prepare for your role as a leader in a matrix organizational structure. What is required of you to be prepared? How will you know when you are ready? These questions will be discussed and expanded upon to put yourself in the best possible position for success in your role.

What is evident is that what got you where you are now is not going to work in your role in a matrix structure. You need to think about building a coalition of key individuals, which happens to be one of the 13 key strategic questions surveyed by our group of leaders who provide insight into the most helpful resources for their jobs. Understanding your unique situation and making the best of important relationships will encourage success in your role and with your team. Relationships are the heart of the project, program, and portfolio manager's job function. Interactions with people at all levels of the organization, within cross-functional groups, and externally will result in spending the proper time and effort to harvest fruitful relationships in which both parties are satisfied.

In your role, what are others' perceptions of you in a matrix environment? Do others treat you as an ally, an equal, or as an obstacle?

How can you best position yourself so others are more willing to cooperate and comply with your requests that come from your management role? Hint: It is not always about what you want or need. Understanding the core values of others and what motivates them will get you much farther than trying hostile tactics.

Project, program, and portfolio managers have many opportunities to volunteer internally in their organization, such as participating in quality groups and steering committees, or externally in professional organizations such as PMI. These opportunities are hidden gems in that they can increase your ability to be influential inside your organization. Through networking, learning new skills, and fostering new and existing relationships, volunteering does play a part in a leader's role in a matrix organization. One of the 13 strategic questions that were asked among the 55 project, program, and portfolio managers was, "Has volunteering played a role in their ability to influence inside their roles in the organization?" Evidence showed over 56% of the group felt volunteer roles play an important part of their ability to influence inside the organization. This author has also personally felt the power of volunteering in professional organizations.

Following are four key contributing factors that will be discussed throughout the book. Situational examples will be provided to better understand these responses. These questions have been gathered through my experiences, with the ultimate goal of trying to guide you to success in your job.

> *Contributing Factor* #1: Does the project, program, or portfolio manager feel that the ability to influence team members, outsiders, and other leaders inside and outside the organization contributes to the success in the leader's role?
>
> *Contributing Factor* #2: Did the project, program, or portfolio manager feel he or she was successful overall in the role of leadership without formal authority?
>
> *Contributing Factor* #3: Was organizational culture a factor in a role of leadership without formal authority in the organization?
>
> *Contributing Factor* #4: Did a role in the organization, past or present, prepare the leader for being in a leadership role without authority?

1

WHAT GOT YOU HERE WILL NOT WORK NOW

The ability to break old habits that can hold you back in a project, program, or portfolio management career is indispensable to the future success of your work. In previous roles where you had formal authority over your team for the various endeavors you managed, you led in a certain way and used a certain type of leadership style that was effective at the time. You may be comfortable with this style and wish to use it in your role in a matrix structure. What this chapter aims to do is to adjust old habits that can get in the way of realization of your project's, program's, or portfolio's goals. Old habits die hard for a reason, and accepting this fact is your first step to learning a new style of leadership. We are going to look at a simple yet effective way of adjusting old habits.

Changing a habit can be broken down to a three-step process. It does not need to be a long, drawn-out experience. In fact it is quite empowering and gratifying. First, make the decision that you are going to stop the undesirable habit. You cannot expect to change unless you put full effort into the process, which means spending as much time as is needed on breaking the undesirable habit. You must believe in what are you doing; otherwise, when the opportunity comes you will revert to your old ways again.

As for step two, it is to put your habit into writing, which makes the process all that more powerful. It makes your goal real, and others can read it. Perhaps make a blog post or post an update on a social networking website so people around you can hold you accountable and are aware of what you are trying to accomplish. Help can come in many forms and having your own team behind you can be powerful. You could also discuss it with members of your team or a fellow project, program, or portfolio manager. They may offer you suggestions and perhaps also went through something similar and can share their story with you. This approach will make the process more comfortable, and there is less chance of resistance to the new behavior.

Finally, step three is a two-part process. First, identify the triggers that make you perform that habit in the first place. By doing so, it will only help you in preventing setbacks. The second part of the third step is self-reflection. This technique has been proven to help people think clearly and make better decisions. You can do this at your desk for a few minutes when you feel the need to break from your tasks. Take the next 5 minutes to think of a habit that you want to break.

Once you are comfortable with this three-step process you can continue reading this chapter.

One of the strategic questions asked to the group of leaders was, "Did you feel you were overall successful in the role of a project, program, or portfolio manager without formal authority over your team?" Nearly half the group, 45%, felt they were either somewhat or not successful in their role. Learning from others that have walked in your shoes is always better than living those experiences on your own. This approach is true just as long as you learn the lesson and apply it to your job; then learning occurs, and you can be assured you are on the right track. With all the resources available to project, program, or portfolio managers, why would nearly half of those surveyed say they were not successful in their role? Some people in the survey may not have been prepared for their role, which will be discussed in Chapter 2 of this book. Preparation is the ultimate key to success. There is no such thing as being too prepared to be a project, program, or portfolio manager in a matrix environment.

Learning effective communication skills is at the core of your job. The majority of your time spent as a project, program, or portfolio manager is in communicating with others, in verbal or written form. Neglecting your team and not regularly "checking in" to listen to their concerns is an example of how you may lose cooperation from your team. What does effective communication look like? I would like you to think for a minute how you would gauge if you were effective in an e-mail you sent to a customer to give them a status update at any given time. Was it quick and to the point? The devil is in the details. Everyone is different, understanding what is important to that person is what will decide if you were successful or not in your e-mail. Taking the time to discuss at the start, what they are expecting in communication methods and details would show not only that you care, but that you can also meet the needs of your team. Once you can meet their needs you can influence them. This is a key point that has to be understood in your role.

This may or may not be your first role as a project, program, or portfolio manager. When you are a leader it is not about you anymore. It is about your team, I repeat, it is about your team. Successful leaders understand this approach, but some have trouble putting this point into practice. Some people want to make all successes that happen in the team about themselves, but this method is not the way to handle the situation. Your team is a reflection of yourself, and you are judged by your peers, your manager, and your clients. Every process and procedure should be directed to your team's success and not to your looking good to your manager or fellow coworkers.

Hoarding of information may work initially to your advantage, but it is not going to get you far. These traits are of unsuccessful leaders that lack the discipline to grow and improve in their job. Discipline is not something that you are born with but is something you acquire over time from trying and failing. Failing is a process on the way to success. Success is not seen as point to point in succession, it is more like zigzagging with some level of setback along the way until you succeed in what you are trying to accomplish. It should be mentioned that how you handle yourself in a setback when no visible progress is being made is what defines you as a leader. A setback is one of the most difficult times as you have no accomplishments to celebrate. Not stopping or quitting but persevering is what will take you to the next step in the process. There is always gold at the end of the rainbow for those that work hard and persevere. Your team members and clients can recognize how you perceive yourself. You need to always be honest and forthcoming and never hide or distort any of the details. Hiding what you may perceive saves your job today limits its progress tomorrow.

There is always a place and need for obtaining support within the organization. It can now be understood that reducing turnover and increasing workplace commitment holds a key position within the organization. When leaders are engaged they are more than likely to carry out leadership functions as well as they are more than willing to stay with the organization when compared to leaders who do not have organizational support from their direct manager and peers. Support is necessary to perform daily functions and to carry out larger cross-functional projects, programs, and portfolios within the organization. When a leader comes up through positions of increasing responsibility their success rate increases while working in a matrix structure.

Support within the organization comes from forming relationships with strategic players. A strategic player is someone who is respected by peers and the management team. They would have peers within the organization going to them for advice and consultation. A strategic player could also be a subject matter expert or have made substantial contribution to the organization.

It must be understood that examining the traits of leaders that are in a position of influence has the same value and importance as learning how to be influential as a leader. Successful leaders look up to other leaders inside and outside the organization in similar positions on a regular basis to improve their knowledge and skill set. It is not necessary to reinvent the wheel in most instances for the leader as they are able to modify past experiences to meet their current and future needs.

Take the next 5 minutes or so to think of leaders who are influential to you, and write down on a piece of paper the qualities they have that you wish to acquire. We are going to use the mind mapping technique to visualize this process. Mind mapping can be just as effective for an individual as in a team setting. Mind mapping for the most part is straightforward, there is not much preparation required to get started on which is favorable to you. What you are going to do is take a piece of paper, draw a circle around a central topic or question and begin connecting subtopics, and keywords to the subtopics. Mind mapping is useful for documenting ideas and acts as a mechanism for brainstorming. Mind mapping helps the individual visually "see" a problem and its possible solutions. Please note, keep all versions of your mind maps for reference when you want to make any changes to your topics or question in the center of the page, it will document your thought process. Mind mapping is successful for seeing the big picture and is an ingredient for successful decision-making processes. Once you are satisfied with your mind map put it aside for now. You are going to refer to the mind map you created throughout the book whenever you feel it is needed. At the start of each chapter, the following mind map (see Figure 1.1) is displayed that this book reinforces in being an influential leader in a matrix structure. It is important to consider all areas of the mind map to be successful as a project, program, or portfolio manager.

This book provides insight into several key questions. These questions are as follows:

- In what ways can a leader gain influence in the workplace?
- What were some roadblocks for those that failed at leading in a matrix structure?
- Besides the ability to influence, what makes a leader successful in a matrix structure?

Understanding these questions is important to the aims that this book tries to achieve. Project, program, and portfolio managers have sought answers to these questions during their careers and these topics will be discussed in detail. It is this author's goal to provide the necessary answers and insight for leaders to accomplish their goals in the workplace.

For a leader to be successful they have to work smart whether they have formal authority over their team or not. There is a certain type of leader that will succeed more and accomplish more in the organization than another. The ability to be agile and to make decisions smartly will ensure success and that objectives are met. Going forward, in Chapter 2 preparing for your leadership role, this book has introduced topics that the research questions asked and enlightened the reader on the topic of being successful at leading people in a matrix organizational structure.

This chapter has outlined several ways project, program, or portfolio managers can break old habits that will interfere with their future success in their role in a matrix environment. Some of the most chronic habits have been outlined in effort to be successful as a leader in a matrix environment. A plan has been identified consisting

Figure 1.1 Mind map of influential leaders.

of self-reflection and alerting people around you who can assist you in the goals that you have outlined and described. Seeking the help of a mentor which can come in many forms for key decision-making and to avoid pitfalls has been identified. Using the mind mapping technique to envision traits you wish to acquire from leaders that you respect is a sure fire way to map your way to success. Chapter 2 will take you through the process of preparing for your leadership role in a matrix environment. It has already been said that overpreparation just adds to the future success of the individual.

SUMMARY CHECKLIST

- Create a list of your undesirable habits.
- Identify triggers for those habits.
- Create a mind map of successful leadership traits you wish to have.
- Commit and start to make lasting changes.
- Tell others of your intentions and goals.
- Celebrate when you have progress!

2

PREPARING FOR YOUR LEADERSHIP ROLE

Looking back at Chapter 1 and the mind map of influential leaders you created, how do you currently stand with your identified skills for improvement, leadership traits, and your overall progress? This mind map will start each chapter to guide what this book teaches and to give you the opportunity to compare your goals and progress along your journey. Always have an open discussion with your group on where you stand, and if you are having any roadblocks (Figure 2.1).

Before undertaking your leadership role in a matrix organizational structure you should commit some time to understand yourself as a professional. There has been much conversation about the advantages of emotional intelligence and decision-making to date. Emotional intelligence means you are not only aware of others emotions, you are aware of your own. This is a skill that for the most part has to be learned through experience and a combination of acquiring knowledge. One should first ask the question, why do I need to be in touch with my own emotions to be a project, program, or portfolio manager? Being able to control your emotions and understand them will make you a more proficient and complete leader. As a more complete leader you will mature your skill set into the most capable leader you can be. You will be leading others and you cannot expect to do so if you cannot lead yourself. You will become more in touch with your team and your client's concerns, as well as resolving problems more effectively as a leader. Furthermore, your team will be a more cohesive group quicker and form stronger bonds, which will increase the quality and output of your work.

The aspect of emotional intelligence that we are going to focus on is self-awareness. There is good reason to focus on this part of emotional intelligence that will be discussed. Although this is the toughest aspect to develop it is among the most worthwhile and potentially

Figure 2.1   Mind map of influential leaders.

useful skill to develop as a project, program, or portfolio manager. Being self-aware teaches the learner that we as individuals have faults; no one is perfect at the end of the day. As a leader, this may be hard to acknowledge, perhaps on the outside the leader has a flawless record. Looking closer, there are situations that could have been handled differently, understanding this and being able to acknowledge shortcomings will only progress your career and likelihood of success in a matrix structure. You also have to cooperate and interact directly and indirectly with members at all different levels of the organization and understanding your faults will help you also improve on your team members' faults also. Allowing for open communication with the team and your manager will provide the ability to accept feedback, which is the key to improving yourself. If you cannot see any need for improvement then chances are that you will not make efforts in professional development. When working in a matrix structure there will be instances where you do not know the best answer but have to make a decision on limited information. Being self-aware will increase the likelihood of success in these situations. In your role chances are that you have been in plenty of situations where there were multiple options available to choose from and none were a clear pick.

One advantage of knowing your strengths and weaknesses is the ability to utilize your team's assets to their full potential. A leader that does not know his or her weakness can never be that successful. Exposing your weakness without some protection is going to leave room for others to take advantage of the situation. Everyone appreciates the ability to contribute to the organization; this is an ideal situation where you can make this happen. Upon starting your role as a project, program, or portfolio manager you should have team-building sessions where the focus is to understand and form relationships with the people you will be working with on a regular basis. Using this time to understand how everyone will contribute to the organization will lead to smoother day-to-day operations; while in stressful times will maintain quality as you manage your work. This also lets you minimize risk and provides for future training needs and goals. Communication and relationships have been mentioned as key components for leaders. It is upon these relationships that your work will be executed. At times your relationships will be tested and it is from strong bonds made earlier that you will weather the storm.

Perhaps one of the hardest things is to see yourself as others see you. We all have some form of blinders and neglect certain aspects of ourselves. We always want to see the brighter and more positive side and less of what needs to be improved. One of the strategic questions asked among the group of project, program, as portfolio managers was, "What did you do to prepare yourself for your management role in a matrix structure?" Figure 2.2 displays the results of the survey question.

We are going to analyze the breakdown of the results. Coming in first, consulting with a peer or manager ranks highest at 35 responses, with a tie of 27 responses each for second place ranking online research and reading magazines proved to be an invaluable resource for leaders embarking on their new role in a matrix structure. All the options but one is self-directed, that is the leader had to initiate the task that best suits his or her needs and personality. Learning to anticipate what you need to learn and how you can best learn the required material will only allow you to be better prepared for these situations. Training has been moved from the human resource department to the line manager and now on to the learners themselves. It is up to the individual to understand and forecast where he or she is headed. Maximizing your

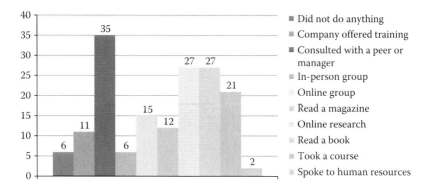

Figure 2.2 Preparation tools for your leadership role. Responses from 55 project, program, and portfolio managers.

effectiveness and managing the information you consume to your benefit will allow you to spend more time on topics that matter to you and your organization. Although this sounds like a daunting task there are many avenues that can be explored that were not available just as short as 5 years ago.

It is no wonder then why consulting with a peer or manager ranks the highest of the available choices. There were only 11 responses out of 55 total for company-sponsored training as a preparation method for leaders. Could this be a fault of the organization, or demands that the requirements are too much and too unique, therefore it is more efficient to have the learner in charge of his or her career learning experiences? It is far more desirable to have customized learning that meets your needs rather than creating a program that tries to group everyone together. There is no one group that can meet the needs of today's leaders. Being industrious, taking initiative in your career is necessary. Find out what learning tools best work for you and the ones that are the most beneficial. Reevaluating these tools on a quarterly to biannual basis and always seeking new innovative ways to obtain information that is more in line with your needs is what is useful for work in a matrix structure.

Joining a local PMI chapter or participating in the online communities of those in other organizations provides many learning opportunities and the ability to network with likeminded peers. Sharing information and tools with those around you will allow others to do the same with what they find helpful and useful. Building coalitions is discussed in Chapter 5. This chapter seeks to illustrate the many ways that you can acquire information and what has been helpful to the group of leaders in this survey. Being prepared takes preparation in itself. Working smart, leveraging individuals and resources around you will enable you to be more knowledgeable and therefore succeed in a matrix structure.

Meeting regularly (weekly or biweekly) with a small group of six to ten professionals that you can be honest with concerning your professional triumphs, future goals, and setbacks will provide the necessary support in your transition period, as well as ongoing on-the-job support and advice for the duration of your career. After all, the number one response was consulting with a peer or manager in preparing for your leadership role. There is much value for all parties involved in the group. Being able to count on your support team when you need to discuss important topics that can assist with your career is worth its weight in gold.

What causes a leader to lose his or her way in a matrix structure? There is always the fear of failure in a new venture that is being undertaken. Fearing failure while in the preparation stages of your new role is normal. You may have reached success in past roles and fear possible setbacks in this new role. Managing your fear through achievable goals and milestones will help you stay focused. There needs to be a fundamental transition from the individual to the collective group in your new role. Operating as an individual that rules with an iron fist and takes little direction from your team will not take you far in the matrix structure. This is one of the quickest ways to unravel your past successes and accomplishments. You will be asked to reach out to others on a regular basis and solicit advice from peers, cross-functional members, and others in the organization that can influence the decision-making for your endeavors. This is where your relationship building skills you have been working on will come into play. This group of individuals will be more than happy to lend a hand when asked for if they are feeling they are a part of the direction and goals of their work. There are many approaches for utilizing institutional knowledge in your decision-making processes and in the planning stages of your work. This knowledge does not come easily, and when it is accessible you should take full advantage of it. Failure to use this knowledge does not further your plans and promotes instability, which is what you do not want do to in your new role.

The transition from the individual to the collective group occurs in the preparation stage of becoming a leader in a matrix structure. Checking your ego at the door and adopting the "WE" mentality will keep your team focused on accomplishing the group mission rather than individual accomplishments. You need to be the role model for your team even though they do not directly report to you, it is not only your responsibility but in your team's interest. Your team still looks up to you for direction and consultation on the tasks they have been given. You are your team's moral compass on how to approach ethical situations. The way a task is completed by the team member is influenced by the way the leader communicates what is important to the individual. Quality, timeliness, and customer satisfaction levels are all being learned from the leader. This question is important that you understand this when you communicate to your team members and provide direction. When you have people looking up to you it puts pressure on you to perform and not look weak to your followers. Every leader faces challenges, and showing weakness is not a fatal flaw but a natural part of leadership. Your team will see you as a person who in fact does have some flaws and is doing his or her best with the information he or she is given. They will be more willing to take risks and innovate, which all leaders hope their team aspires to accomplish.

You need to understand you are going to be empowering others to lead and in turn take responsibility for their actions. This transfer of responsibility is empowering for your team members and can drive improvements in your work that were not there before. Utilizing the empowerment of others is what successful leaders do in a matrix structure. These leaders recognize they may not have formal authority, but when they empower others to act they get the results they are seeking. Learning from others and treating your team as equals increases the respect you are given by your team. When your team respects you, it highly increases the likelihood they will follow your orders and the mission of the organization and that of your desired goals. This concept seems straightforward but it can take a long time to be fully realized for some. Learning how to be a good listener means more than just providing people with a platform to talk and get their point across; it means helping them realize their ideas. Your job is to coordinate, facilitate, and direct the discussions of your team in the direction you set in a matrix structure. You need to be careful that you do in fact have a genuine interest in their ideas and are willing to oversee them into fruition. If your interests are not genuine you need to communicate this with your group and correct this problem. Your team is quite capable of recognizing it if you are not genuinely interested in their comments and welfare. This is a sign that you are heading on the wrong track of your leadership role and can be the start of a number of problems that teams face. Guiding the direction through inspiration and commitment will solidify the path your team will take when you are the leader.

In your role in a matrix organization structure you will do a substantial amount of communicating with individuals at all levels of the organization. Learning how to be comfortable speaking in groups and making presentations will help you get your point across when you are in these situations. Joining a local Toastmaster group, for example, where you can practice your public speaking abilities, will undoubtedly improve your presentation skills and will lessen the pressure of performing in front of others when needed. These settings are supportive, and everyone is trying to improve their public speaking while at the same time helping others in the group so they are in the same situation you are in. Toastmaster groups are a proven structure for improving public speaking and communication skills in a small group setting. To learn more about this organization go to its website at www.toastmasters.org and find a club near you. It is amazing how a little work on one's public speaking can improve one's delivery and communication skills. It helps in using body language in communicating in person and being more engaging with those that are listening. Engagement in the workplace may not always be easy, and there are situations where the audience is difficult and the additional effort from a Toastmasters group can help immensely.

Unlearning undesirable behaviors that you picked up along your career is difficult, and without a path to take that leads to success, you may end up not advancing further. Using this chapter to discuss with your group and remedy situations you were in, that could have been handled differently by you or someone else will only prepare yourself for your upcoming role as a project, program, or portfolio manager in a matrix structure. Where do these undesirable traits come from? Why would leaders not do things the right way all the time? There is much to be said for taking the easy way out when no one is watching or you have the authority to do so. Poor behaviors are perceived as the easier way to perform a task. I say perceived as doing the wrong thing means you have to undo the action and redo it the right way, *eventually*. This always takes longer to redo what could have been done the right way the first time. Not giving in to the wrong way over time will make it easier to stay on the right path. Once you stop and take a short cut you have to start all over again. Being in a team environment where others will pick up on your poor behavior and decrease your efforts means as a leader you will need to be more than cautious of your actions. Training your team to be honest, and taking the necessary time to complete a task, provides the foundation for success. Also keep in mind, when you are working with cross-functional teams you are the face of the work.

When there is a crisis in leadership there is virtually always a crisis in followership. Losing a percentage of your followers is something that all leaders dread happening as they know how hard it is to get people on board with your agenda and contribute to the goal. Unfortunately it does happen, more than one wants to admit at times. Why do followers stop following the leader? Much could be said for the leader not instilling common goals, listening, and implementing followers' needs. What it comes down to is that followers have a choice to follow the leader. If the followers see in the leader what they view as in their favor, they will follow the leader's path. Regaining followers as a leader in a matrix structure is difficult as your interactions can be limited to key individuals. Working with individuals in other departments limits your influence, as does working with remote teams. The leader is in a much better position to continually be campaigning for followers, than to wait when there is a problem due to a crisis. Getting over a crisis puts the advantage on the side of the leader to keep and gain new followers. Increase in communication from leader to followers and transparency play a key role in crises. People always want to know what is happening and having systems in place that serve to share information in a way that is easy to understand and follow will be in the leader's favor.

Leadership should be viewed as a process and a dynamic relationship. Leadership takes place within groups. It is the job of the leader to provide the path to take, clarify goals, and facilitate communication within the group and with outsiders. Leadership is much more than displaying and using authority. By solely relying on authority, the leader is limiting the group in its overall success and effectiveness, not to mention innovation! This is where some less skilled and experienced leaders fall into the authority trap. Once you rely on fear, you drastically limit how far your team can go, and the goals they can collectively achieve. If you feel this may be part of your leadership style discuss it with your group. You will be surprised on the views of a leader relying on authority and fear in their role. This is a good opportunity for growth and understanding on how to create a high-performance team environment. Your views may be challenged, and you need to keep an open mind in this situation.

Although a project, program, or portfolio manager in a matrix organization structure does not necessarily have formal authority over his or her team, it would be naive to think authority is all that is needed to manage and delegate successfully within the team. Authority, although inadequate for most situations, does have a place in organizations. Knowing how much authority should be exercised is an art, as much as it is a skill. When in doubt, always go one step below in terms of demands on others. Displaying and exercising authority is something that should be fine-tuned through applying past experiences. Seasoned leaders know that authority distorts relationships and creates an unequal balance among individuals when overemphasized. Project, program, or portfolio managers that are in tune with their leadership style will be most effective when using authority over team members or external resources. This book assumes that the majority of leaders could have little or no formal authority over his or her team and needs to use more tact to sway and align others on the team. Trying to keep the balance equal with resources and individuals in other departments or group is a complex task. Reevaluating and improving on your tactics on politeness and the general ability to make someone feel important and delighted can go quite far in getting what you want. People have been known to go out of their way when someone takes the time to ask them for assistance and says thank you afterward with a personalized note.

Far too often, we use the term *leader* synonymously with commander. A leader that lets the team take turns steering under the leader's supervision is just as much as a leader that steers the ship on his or her own. Part of being a leader is grooming team members to take on more responsibility and leadership roles within the team. What better opportunity to test the waters when there is someone helping and guiding, explaining actions taken and answering questions along the way. Your support group can play an integral role when trying it out in the workplace. This provides the leader with an understanding of the skills, knowledge, and competencies his or her team members have in their roles and he or she can counter this with their knowledge and experience. The leader cannot solely rely on himself or herself to steer the team in a matrix structure. A team that is part of the decisions, large or small, is one that shares a bond and will weather difficult times together better.

A leader that is disciplined will go farther and longer, with superior results than those that lack this critical skill. Discipline primarily comes through experience. Laziness is a great enemy of discipline; the same is the case for other forms of inefficiency. A leader that lacks discipline magnifies the effect on their team tenfold through osmosis. Obtaining self-efficiency in communication and calendar management can mean saving time to improve current processes and stay ahead of the plan as a project, program, or portfolio manager. A project, program, or portfolio manager in an average day communicates with others in short bursts of communication a great deal of the time and not knowing how to maximize and better utilize their own and the team's time can be the start of a magnitude of problems that can be faced in project, program, and portfolio management. Creating or improving on a system that your team can use to communicate will only make your role easier to manage.

What kind of a leader are you? There are two basic types. There are transactional leaders, who exchange one thing for another, and there is transformation leadership that seeks to engage others to their full ability as followers. Understanding this difference and transitioning to the transformational style if you need to will help you when you want to explore options to improve your leadership skills on the job as a leader. This will also help you understand others that you work with either on a regular basis or infrequent basis. You still have to put the same level of effort for each type. Effort requires time, and time is limited. Knowing this, make best use of your communications with other leaders and your team members on every occasion. By having an understanding and plan of action to address what is important to them will ensure mutual benefit amongst all parties.

By now, you should have a good sense of the preparation that is required for your new role from the material discussed in this chapter thus far. Where do you see your best results in the new role? Where do you think you need to spend some more time, and dedicate the necessary time and resources to overcome the necessary hurdles to ensure success in a matrix environment? A principle known as the Pareto principle also known as the 80-20 rule that shows that 80% of the effects come from 20% of the causes. Finding what can be called your sweet spot, *your* 20% and seeking to maximize its effect and gain share is should be your goal. What do you do really well that you can rely on for your future role? Write a list of five to seven items of areas you excel in and those that require improvement. There are goals that you clearly need to work on but that will take longer than your preparation period to starting the role. How will you handle this and address these concerns? These long-term goals need to be addressed and time spent on them, but your skills are what will determine the majority of your success in the role. Discussing with your group how to minimize the effects of your weaknesses that will be worked on in the long term is the best path to take.

Most of the best investments an individual can make are long term and require moderate-to-high levels of sacrifice to achieve. Without the sacrifice and difficulty you would not have already acquired the said knowledge. Accepting the fact that you will struggle and initially suffer in some areas of your life to achieve your goals will help you commit and concentrate on achieving them. Once you achieve one goal, the next one is a bit easier than the first, and so on. Of course there is always the difficulty at the onset of the commitment. I call this the price you have to pay, and everyone has to pay it, either upfront with effort or overtime with poor results. There are no short cuts, as short cuts do not last and never achieve the same levels that require dedication. People around you will see your commitment and encourage you to go further. You may even reciprocate and support them in their own unique set of challenges in their career. The small group that you built is an integral part of your journey. I hope by now your team is proving some returns, and they are assisting you to prepare for your project, program, or portfolio management role. They do not all need to be leaders themselves, but their intentions must be genuine and their goals and values should be similar to yours.

This book, as you must be aware of by now, is not full of trends or quick fixes to succeed or be a competent leader. The approach has always been that of a close friend guiding you along your career as a project, program, or portfolio manager. With the results of the analytical survey of the 13 strategic questions, you as the reader gain from multiple perspectives on important topics for your upcoming role. This has been the design as is the group you have selected that counsels you and can provide guidance beyond this book. Trust + preparation × courage is the formula in this book. It is with smaller steps in preparation that in practice we can take those giant leaps, which are paramount to growth. Never let what is important become urgent in your preparation or an on-the-job training regimen.

The more essential the role of the leader, the less effective he or she is to the group and company, this has to be understood. A person can only stretch oneself so thin before problems arise and one's work is in jeopardy. In the following chapters, you will learn how to build a coalition and spread the responsibility among your direct and extended team members. Adopting this mindset early on will only make it more powerful when you take action as a project, program, or portfolio manager in a matrix structure. Relying on others that you do not have authority over can be a scary concept for some, but there is much you can do to reduce the risk. In fact, it is up to you to determine how much you can rely on others for your workload. How does one start relying on others when they have not done this before? Taking small steps on topics that are in a side position to more important items is the key. Learning involves making adjustments and failing from time to time. When there is not much risk involved in the request, you will feel more comfortable at first taking these key steps in improving your leadership skills. Communicating to the person and asking for feedback will further assist you. Once you hear how the other person thought you acted, you can reflect and make any adjustments. Over time leaning on your team for tasks that have merit will become second nature. This is how you can grow your team and develop their own skill sets. Building trust is an investment, one that is required in high-functioning teams.

Now that you are learning to trust and rely on others in your day-to-day operations as a project, program, or portfolio manager, we can discuss the topic of how to handle blame. The leader takes responsibility and fixes the problem at hand. Leaders do not seek to be quick to blame or point fingers. You are the leader, it is your responsibility, period. By providing your team with the most accurate information to accomplish a task you are decreasing the chances of error. A team that trusts each other will work together and try to help others on the team when possible. Purposely withholding information to gain authority over others is not going to last long and will end quickly. Those that rely on authority are the worst leaders and the most common in the business world. Aim to go higher than average; you worked far too hard to be average.

As a leader in a matrix structure, you will be working with people of different educational backgrounds and varied years of experience in the industry. Learning how to campaign for recent college and university graduates as followers is a way to ensure a lengthy followership. These individuals tend to be more than willing to listen to words of experience if it can help them in their day-to-day tasks in their jobs. When you are there for them, they will be there for you. This is a reciprocal relationship, where two parties exchange things of mutual value. Reciprocity is discussed in detail in further chapters so more information on the topic is forthcoming. This is one of the key tactics and groups that are to your advantage in your new role seeing you are without formal authority over your team members. Although there is something to be said for speaking to the most experienced person in the room, having a group of eager individuals that can be helpful is positive. Often these people report to subject matter experts, and you can get additional information from them. Learning how to be creative as just demonstrated is par for the course for a matrix structure. There are no direct *a* to *b* relationships, and the matrix approach requires a different route to obtain the needed information. Creativity to some may not be their best skill set, as they may be more analytically inclined, but it is not something that cannot be learned, with sincere effort.

How you portray the work that is to be performed by your team and resources directly affects the effort and quality that is put in the work itself. You empower your team to do work activities and expect results in return, often in a hurry. When those results lack quality, you need to know why. It is not acceptable to place blame on the individual, except to correct the action itself. Your work is to be treated with the utmost respect, and those working on it should be equally respected. How do you respect work activities? Allocating adequate time, resources, and having someone that is competent on the topic do the work is a start. When your team sees that you respect the work they will feel respected also as individuals. Much of respect and working with someone involves mutual reciprocity. If the individual feels he or she lacks respect and trust, the person may not put forth the best effort to complete assigned activities. This is to be expected.

Processes establish rules and guidelines. How will you approach this new role versus the one of your previous position? Do you envision processes being much different? Are there any similarities? Not having formal authority can ruin your plans if you let it, and it is important to recognize this before you start your role. How can you safeguard yourself and your work under these new or modified processes? Is there a standard guideline already in place, or are you going to have to create one yourself? This is an opportunity to get several people in the organization to answer these questions when you start your role. It should be understood that what gets measured gets done in the workforce. This is just the way things are for most people.

Doors open to new opportunities when we confront our doubts and fears. Throughout this chapter you should be breaking new ground and striving for growth. Taking steps in unfamiliar territory is the only way you are going to grow as a leader and individual. Growth is not easy, it never has been, and you need to focus on key skills that you can grow or develop. Tell yourself this uncomfortable feeling you are having is only temporary, which it is. You will soon become skilled in the subject or desire you are trying to achieve. Now, I want you to count the number of improvements you are working on at this moment and cut that number in half. You should only be working on two to four aspects of your leadership skill set at a time. They require the appropriate level of dedication and time respectively. You cannot coordinate half a dozen or more improvement projects concurrently and get stellar results. Once you accomplish a goal start on another. Focusing on key improvement areas will allow you to truly reach new ground and break limits that you had before.

This chapter may frighten you, in the sense that you are working on areas of yourself that may have been dormant for a long period of time or require improvement. What you need to tell yourself, is that what you are feeling is temporary, and you can get through this, as you have gotten through difficult situations in the past. You can overcome adversity and break new paradigms in your leadership and management thinking. It is not sufficient to make small steps in your progress; you need to take giant leaps to succeed. No individuals that made small steps after steps made much for themselves in their industry. It is the leaders and innovators that dominate the landscape in the business world. You too can become a leader and an innovator, if you believe in your abilities and make the first move to success. Life gives the test first and provides the lesson afterward. You will continue to progress and grow throughout this book through all chapters. This chapter has solely been to prepare you for what is coming by providing some guidance and knowledge that will suit most people as intended.

It is in preparation that we get to recognize the areas in us in need of improvement and prepare ourselves for the challenges that will face us in the future. At this stage you should be comfortable with what you need to do to prepare and ask of others including your group. While these individuals will be supporting you, it is up to you to take the lead and steer the ship to its destination that you want to head. No one knows you better than yourself. Long-time colleagues or friends may be able to provide assistance in critical areas, but it is your desire and goals that will ultimately see yourself succeed or fall short of the mark. Working in a matrix organization requires working with many people at different levels and departments in the organization. You need to be able to lead on your own with minimal assistance and lead others in your team to direct and control your work. Becoming comfortable with the feeling of leading yourself and others when you are unsure of the steps to take at all times comes with practice. This chapter provides this needed practice for you in an environment that is supportive and provides feedback to improve.

The next chapter discusses understanding your organizational structure. Now that you have a better understanding of yourself, you are able to appreciate the greater picture and examine the organization, where you fit within it and the projects, programs, or portfolios you manage. Understanding others that you will interact with on an ongoing basis in the organizational structure will also help you in leveraging them to your advantage when needed. It is not sufficient to just campaign for followers in your team, but reaching out and casting a larger net within the organization and beyond is necessary. Individuals outside the organization can prove to be indispensable for knowledge and for utilizing resources. It will be discussed in the chapter, that knowing how to "work" your LinkedIn account, for example, and utilizing its full potential cannot be underestimated. The meta-data that LinkedIn provides to its members is astonishing. It is also a proven and popular central location through which you can manage your followers. There is no substitution for face-to-face discussions, but they are not always available, so you must make to do with what you have. Social media may not be the vehicle of choice for your network, but it has its merit and when leveraged properly, can greatly play into the leader's favor. Organizations are using tools, such as Microsoft's Yammer, to bring social networking into the workplace have proven to be widespread and beneficial by almost every industry.

No two organizations are the same, but they do have similarities and unique attributes that can be studied and understood. Studying your organizational structure will show how communication flows, is disassembled, and processed by others. Making meaningful communication and directing others takes effort and experience to do it well, with precision and excellence. In this chapter you learned how to prepare for your leadership role and you are finding out that it takes more time and effort than you might have thought initially. Learning how to be efficient and effective at the same time will allow you the necessary time that it takes to manage your followers and coalitions appropriately.

Your level of efficiency and effectiveness as a project, program, or portfolio manager has been challenged and will continue for the duration of this book. Many techniques have been discussed so far that can be implemented in your new role. For the longer-term self-improvements, having a starting point that you can monitor for future success will only assist in seeing these longer-term goals into fruition and make a meaningful impact on the work you manage and your role within the organization.

You are learning what it takes to be a leader in a matrix organizational structure. It takes time, effort, and has setbacks that can be managed effectively. Perhaps it is harder than you thought it would be, but be assured that this book will assist you in your quest with your peers and other leaders. No goal that was worthwhile accomplishing came easy and without sacrifice. It is in the sacrifice and in the learning that you grow and improve as a leader and then become what your organization requires.

SUMMARY CHECKLIST

- Think about better understanding yourself as a leader and what changes you need to make to improve.
- Understand your self-awareness skill as a leader and see if it can be improved.

- Join a professional community, online or in person, such as Project Management Institute (PMI).
- Build your group of six to ten professionals and commit to meet regularly (weekly/biweekly).
- Need to improve public speaking? Try joining a local Toastmasters group in your area.

.

3

UNDERSTANDING YOUR
ORGANIZATIONAL STRUCTURE

Looking back at Chapter 1 and the mind map of influential leaders you created, how do you currently stand with your identified skills for improvement, leadership traits, and your overall progress? This mind map will start each chapter to guide insight from this book and will give you the opportunity to compare your goals and progress along your journey. Always have an open discussion with your group of six to ten professionals on where you stand and if you have any roadblocks (Figure 3.1).

If someone asks you what an organization is, what would you tell them? What does it mean to you? It can be best defined as a collective group of people systematically arranged to meet a need or obtain an ongoing goal. An organization structure is a framework that shows others the lines of authority, dictates formal communication channels, and allocates duties and rights to individuals. How does the organization structure impact the goal of the company? How does the structure affect the role of a project, program, or portfolio manager? Are there ways a project, program, or portfolio manager can maneuver and succeed in any organization structure? These questions have merit and will be discussed in this chapter.

What makes one choose a particular organizational structure over another? There are times when multiple structures may have merit, but only one can be selected. Understanding the makeup of your organization structure will only work in your favor. There are four major factors that affect an organization's structure: technology, strategy, human resources, and the organizational environment. These factors determine the organizational structure that will be used for the organization. Aligning the strategy with the direction your firm is headed will allow for smoother operations for example. This direction comes from top management with the involvement of the entire management

Figure 3.1   Mind map of influential leaders.

team. Managers often work tirelessly to maintain the course set forth by the strategic direction and goals of the organization.

The quicker the organizational environment changes, the more flexibility is needed for managers and leaders to control the change. This means the more problems they face the more room is needed to adjust their plans and people they manage. It should be noted that technology often is viewed as the golden ticket to the problems that they are facing. In fact, the more technology implemented the harder it is to regulate the organization. Perhaps you worked in such environment in the past or presently. It is a challenge indeed. When planning out work, the manager needs to make use of effective job design in which they group tasks into specific jobs. This makes for an efficient and effective workforce.

As a leader, a matrix organizational structure can be unclear and inefficient to work in at times. This is in part due to the lack of information on what each person's role is in the structure. As a leader you are going to be working with colleagues at all levels of the organization, and it is paramount that you are able to understand and work within the matrix structure without complications. The sooner you become aware of the possible challenges and opportunities for your team the more time you can spend on the most important aspects of your work. Having clarity, design and details of the intentions of a matrix structure will allow you to operate at an efficient and effective pace, with little confusion. This chapter will provide this necessary logic map and insight of the structure you will be working in and provide key aspects that must be recognized by the manager for greater effectiveness.

Because of the complex interdependencies of a matrix structure, the lack of detail and clarification of "who does what" an understanding has to be in place among the various team members and functional managers that the project, program, or portfolio manager will interface with on a regular basis. An obvious answer to the lack of clarity has to be having detailed roles and responsibilities for all team members. Having a "living" document that holds this important information will assist everyone and save time and rework by having the correct lines of communication and flow of information. Spending adequate time to maintain and keep only the most current records on file will prove invaluable to you and your team. There has to be a balance between detail and functionality for this document. If it is too detailed and cumbersome no one will use it; likewise, if it is lacking key information it will only magnify the problem.

What is included in this document? The following is a list of relationships in a matrix structure:

- Far-reaching area of responsibility
- Upper reporting relationship with management
- Horizontal relationships
- Core accountabilities

3.1 Far-Reaching Area of Responsibility

A question that will come up in your role in the developing stages or perhaps far into it is, just how far should you reach out within the organization? How large an impact do you think you can you reasonably make within the organization? Furthermore, how do you know when taking on too much is harmful for you and your projects, programs or portfolios? Some brainstorming should be done such as consulting with key members of your team discussing your intentions and obtaining their ideas.

Once you commit to yourself, others and your team it is often difficult to retract your position. Taking on areas of reasonability such that you can provide a meaningful contribution and impact within the organization is what you as a leader should strive to achieve. Overtaking areas that you cannot adequately control or monitor will most likely not lead to much success or progress in improvements. Failing in this area and the other areas of relationships in a matrix structure can impact your level of influence and ability to get others to cooperate with you when you need them to.

Knowing how to strike a balance comes from experience and from past attempts of marking out areas of reasonability. This process requires diplomacy and knowledge of the functions of the organization. Discussing with those with whom you will be interacting with in the areas in question will answer some of the questions you may have by now. If you are in a new role, first master that and then seek to expand. Always remember, you need to master your domain before you take on others. Once you are at around 90% competency in your domain it is advisable to seek to expand your reach where possible. Following this simple plan will prevent the unnecessary and undesirable effects of taking on too much with either the lack of knowledge or resources to do an acceptable job.

Damaging your reputation is a reality by being unprepared or overstepping your reach in an organization and with clients; it is often not reversible and will follow you. This may take some time to go through several cycles of projects, programs or portfolios to get back to the state they were at previously. Taking this topic seriously and understanding that taking on what you can and learning to say no when necessaey will prove invaluable to you in your career.

3.2 Upper Reporting Relationship with Management

A project, program, or portfolio manager has to on occasion report on issues, risks, progress and status for example to management. Displaying diplomacy and tact, not to mention managing effectively and bringing up the right data to those that make key decisions, will benefit your work and career. Much like understanding your own far-reaching area of reasonability this can come with experience, but there are steps that can be taken immediately to improve this area. Nurturing relationships for a leader does not stop with clients and team members. Executives in the organization play a key role in your success. Building lasting relationships in this area will enable future opportunities and career possibilities for you as a project, program, or portfolio manager.

Relationships with upper managers are about high-level conversations and reporting data about your work so management can make decisions, short range and long term. Knowing what is expected, what people look for, and want will only work in your favor. Summarizing multiple paragraphs in documents, for example, will let the person get a quick glance of what is being discussed. Customizing your relationships with each individual in management that you interact with is no different than with any of your other stakeholders. Leaders require support of the senior management team to be successful. Working at your relationship with management over time will allow better operational support and cross-department support, which are so crucial to a leader. When a situation arises that only management can assist with they will be more inclined to cooperate and work with you on this issue.

The flow of information will mostly be one directional from you to senior management. Feedback from management should be provided on a regular basis. Learning and adapting to your audience is not a new idea for project, program, or portfolio managers. We do it all the time in our roles, and reporting to management is no exception. If management prefers e-mails over in-person meetings, just as long as all needs are met you should accommodate each stakeholder in those situations. The project, program, or portfolio manager is the person that has to accommodate others' needs at times to ensure collaboration and keep the dynamics of the group intact.

There is a five-step process which you can follow to determine the information needs of your stakeholders in detail. This process is called a stakeholder analysis and is now going to be discussed. First, identify all possible stakeholders not filtering to a key few. A stakeholder can be an individual or group, keep this in mind. Second, determine the importance of each stakeholder in an ordered list. You can have flags for marking specific stakeholders as low or high importance. Spending a great deal of time with stakeholders that are not of great importance and not spending enough time with those that are critical to you and your teams success can be easily seen. Third, you need to identify the interest of each stakeholder. They are going to have different interests from each other. Knowing this you can properly pitch ideas and ask for the right support from the correct people and groups. The fifth step is short but can take much time to accomplish. This step is to gain agreement from your stakeholders when it is asked for and needed. Making sure they understand what is expected from you not just informally but in writing. An e-mail will suffice for this with a follow up in person or on the phone. Finally, keep the stakeholder activities within your project workplan. Do not have a separate document for this. At a minimum keep a track of time frames and estimated effort with the responsible person.

3.3 Horizontal Relationships

How do you interact with individuals that are on the same level as you within the organization but may be in different groups or teams? Not being able to rely on formal authority or positional power, the leader has to seek out alternatives to achieve cooperation from the horizontal relationships. If the other person(s) is not cooperating, this can be difficult for the leader to work with on a regular basis. This section discusses how to handle such relationships within the organization.

What is a horizontal relationship and how can you recognize it within the organization? Horizontal relationships are ones that involve two or more people at the same level within the organization and are in either different departments or groups. These can be individuals that you have to collaborate regularly as part of their job functions. There is a formal and an informal component of horizontal relationships that is advantageous to the leader. The formal aspect is having discussions, collaborating and seeing work move forward. The informal component can be social interactions and team-building activities. This informal component should not be overlooked and underdeveloped by the leader. This is where you can build lasting bonds between individuals in horizontal relationships.

The need for teamwork has increased in organizations in the twenty first century, creating opportunities for those who recognize and take advantage of them; strive to be an innovator in this area. The more time you work at either the formal or informal aspect the other aspect will improve as well. Utilizing social networking to maintain your network of relationships is no different for horizontal relationships. Maintaining social networks in corporations requires more than the 9-5 attitude. Understanding this, being able to dedicate set amounts of time for team building with the project team will increase the effectiveness of your relationships at work including the horizontal ones.

3.4 Core Accountabilities

The guidelines discussed for relationships are the main aspects that can be applied to virtually every organization. Perhaps you have unique circumstances and will add to this list if your situation does not fit within the framework. Understanding relationships is paramount to working in matrix organizational structures. This is not new information for the leader whose main function is defined by working within differ-ent relationship hierarchies and formats. It is now evident through the four point guidelines presented in this chapter that there is much to be understood and learned though relationships. By having a project, program, or portfolio manager maintain these living project-related documents will allow the team members to be more self-sufficient and not have to rely on others so much. These documents can be quite empowering for the individual, which should be the goal of every proj-ect, program, and portfolio manager. Time freed up is time that can be spent on more meaningful ior impactful aspects of your work. A leader should always strive to look for time-saving techniques where possible.

As a leader ask yourself how have you managed these relationships and information in the past? If you have a system already in place a slight modification may be needed but use what works for you and your team. Proposing guidelines that are restrictive can do more harm than they try to prevent. Allowing for ambiguity and overlap is acceptable. You may want to have a few brainstorming sessions with your team about these four points and see what diverse views from the team can help you in coming up with a solution that everyone can work with and manage.

Getting buy-in and acceptance is just as important as the policies themselves; never underestimate this aspect. Buy-in is what makes the policy come to fruition and stick in place. Having policies that no one understands or follows can cause the opposite effect desired by the leader. You may be all too familiar with policies of the moment from manage-ment that you had in the past. This dilutes the effectiveness of future policies which should be noted. Do some research on topics that are most important to you and your team(s). Understand in detail the inter-dependencies of these four points. Becoming more of a subject matter expert in relationships such as how to negotiate with horizontal relation-ships will only benefit you and your team. This comes through experi-ences and can be taught to those who wish to take the time to learn the skill sets required for effectiveness. Relationships admittedly come easier for some, while others have to work at them on a regular basis. Over time they can come easier and less forced to those that put in the effort.

Now, this book is going to discuss some strategies for success in matrix structures that can be applied to your organization and team. Having support from senior management is particularly important given that either project, program, or portfolio managers may not be as influential as the managers that are allocating staff. Having a team that is adequately supported and rewarded and recognized will allow for greater levels of success. It has been discussed how to manage relationships with senior management more efficiently and effectively. Take this knowledge and put it to use within your organizational setting.

Interestingly one can ask the question, is hierarchy the opponent of creativity? Why do we need hierarchy in organizations? What is the purpose and what will I get out of it? Does hierarchy shutdown creativity and shut down a sense of ownership for the leader? This question has been asked by many in organizations that are seeking to understand their role and how to work in the organizational structure. The next few paragraphs will discuss this topic of hierarchy in the organization and shed light for you the leader.

3.5 Is Hierarchy the Problem?

It has been said on numerous occasions that the hierarchy in organizations is the reason the leader cannot accomplish a task under the desired constraints. Why is this the case? Why does hierarchy have a bad reputation from those in the organization? Why is it a problem in the first place and why was it not resolved a long time ago? What can be done about it by the manger in order to be more effective? What can senior management do to improve this situation? We will now discuss the hierarchical solution.

3.6 The Hierarchical Solution

Hierarchy enables senior management to direct an employee's behavior, dictate the flow of information within the organization, maintain a degree of control, and steer the organization in the direction the CEO desires to accomplish the organization's strategic goals. How does an organization maintain employee engagement and satisfaction with such model? There is implied inequality within a hierarchy. Those few at the top have the power, and the many at the bottom feel as if they have little to no input within the organization. Such problems can lead to employee tardiness and poor communication within and outside the organization. This inequality can be combated with the use of employee empowerment.

The empowerment model implies accountability built in for the leader. It is a model that accounts for the leader having to follow up and be responsible in an organization that is going to see it grow to its potential and its expectations. You will not develop as a leader in a model of hierarchy and have the best results. What you will do is take the enthusiasm out of a business that has the innovative spirit. By influencing decision-makers and being the example of an accountable leader you can show the vision and the roadmap your department and organization should take.

Having employee empowerment within the organization is one method to lower employee turnover. Greater satisfaction with the employees' work and care will come into place. Quality will improve, and management will have more resources to spend on growing the business rather than having to deal constantly with dissatisfied employees. Employee empowerment is not a one-time event; it is ongoing and is monitored by senior management. Monitoring empowerment effectiveness requires parameters that are not complex in nature and are easily recognizable. Aim for a five point plan for monitoring employee engagement. Having an open dialogue with employees on their needs as well as the needs of the business will aid in creating strong lasting empowerment in the workforce.

The project, program, or portfolio manager works collaboratively with the functional manager, management and the team members to bring about empowerment. This is part of the leader's responsibilities. Not taking this responsibility will impact your work negatively. A five-step model to follow to gain empowerment and how to empower your team is as follows. It starts with knowledge, you need to know the systems involved, understand the dynamics you might encounter and the resources required, and of course you need a plan of action. Second, you need to be able to believe you can accomplish the goal you created. You need to strive to be self-efficient. Third, competence plays a large part in empowering yourself and others. The better your skills and those of your team(s) the greater the competence. The fifth step is a two part step, first is action, being able to take the plans and make things happen while the second part is impact. The process of empowerment is not an overnight change but comes from refining your efforts and striving to be more self-sufficient.

3.7 Horizontal or Flat Organizational Structures

This structure is characterized by few levels of management, open communication and more channels of communication than in a hierarchal structure. In a flat organization employees are not as restricted to their department managers and have more responsibility and decision-making power. Employee satisfaction tends to be greater in these structures. As an example project managers who earlier worked in a hierarchal structure and are now coming to a flat structure will be in for some noticeable changes when entering the organization. There is less need for approvals by management, often leaving the decision-making to the employees themselves. Those that are used to more formal practices will have to adapt to a more nimble organizational structure.

Is there one organizational structure that is optimal and more beneficial than the others? This depends on what kind of organization you are working in. For government and large companies the hierarchy structure is taking a backseat as many organizations have gone towards a less hierarchical approach. The flat structure has received much praise for its design, lack of management layers and employee feedback. There is always a place for each structure and looking to work smart within yours is what your plan should be.

To better understand your organizational structure, refer to key organization documents. These are the corporate mission statement, corporate vision or strategic plan and the corporate values documents. Vision and values differ for each organization. The values are what the organization practices with its employers, vendors, and customers. Vision is where the senior management team is aiming for the company to be. There is no better way to know how to handle a situation than to know what the organization expects of you. These documents may have been given to you when you joined the organization. Inquire if there are any updated documents since then. How does your organization expect you to act? What is important to the organization? Is it ethics, trust or autonomy? Knowing this key information will provide you with the necessary tools in dealing with team members and other members of the organization. It may be a good idea, if you feel it will be beneficial, to review the documents and see with the team how your project fits in with them.

Finally, there is much importance that has to be placed on organizational design and structure. Without a workable design people may be in roles that are dysfunctional. Examples could be lack of coordination, not sharing details, or an inadequate flow of information to list a few. Why would an organization have a poorly designed structure? Perhaps at one point it was a traditional hierarchy which then flattened out or became a matrix. The problem is when the hierarchy remains within the organization after the shift to a new structure. This could because of a lack of knowledge or no processes to ensure that the new hierarchy is followed. As a project, program, or portfolio manager, you often have to do cross-functional work with other groups or teams. You may be putting yourself in positions of chaos and confusion. Being able to recognize this and adapt under the circumstances will ensure your work stays intact.

3.8 The Six Bases of Power

As a leader, you need to understand where power comes from within an organization in order to succeed. Working in a matrix structure does not imply a limitation for you to use certain power within the organization, even though you may not have formal authority over your team members. These powers and others will be discussed in this section. Being able to see what power is being used in a situation will only benefit you in your role as a leader. Those that have to work with difficult people will be especially benefit from this section. Once you understand how someone operates you know how to react, decreasing any stress or uncertainty that may exist within the situation. According to Raven (1993), there are six bases of power: coercive and reward power, legitimate power, expert and referent power and information power. Being able to recognize each base of power the project, program, or portfolio manager can better understand influence, and where it comes from. Each power will now be discussed.

3.8.1 Coercive Power and Reward Power

These two powers come in "personal forms. Going beyond tangible rewards and real physical threats, we have had to recognize that personal approval from someone whom we like can result in quite powerful reward power; and rejection or disapproval from someone whom we really like can serve as a basis for powerful coercive power (Raven and Kruglanski, 1970). There is some indication that the more personal forms, which have sometimes been called 'attraction power,' are more likely to be associated with women than with men" (Broverman et al., 1972; Johnson, 1976).

B. H. Raven, 1993

Looking deeper at coercive power, this power tries to produce fear in others. It is the "stick," compared to reward power, which can be viewed as the "carrot" of the rewards mechanisms. Coercive power requires good judgment by the individual that holds it. Leaders in some instances are expected to be coercive to their subordinates. Coercive power is tested all the time by leaders by forcing subordinates to obey an order or face punishment. As a leader you should seek to be respected by your followers, managers and other leaders in the organization. When you manage with fear alone you bring up some potential problems. As an example, first you would have to ensure compliance 100% of the time rather than followers freely going along with your commands if they respected your decisions and demands. Ensuring compliance 100% of the time is a time intensive task that, when tried, never can be met. However, lacking formal authority in the organization limits your use of this type of power and makes you rely or other sources such as respect and acquiring trust in others.

Reward power simply means giving some type of reward to the employee as a means to influence that person to cooperate and do what is asked of him or her. Being creative, reward power can be quite powerful but if you are using monetary rewards to gain cooperation they can become costly. A plan of action can be brainstorming up mostly nonmonetary rewards and presenting them to employees and seeing if you can agree upon those rewards for cooperation. Use the rewards strategically, by understanding what the employees want will ensure greater cooperation.

3.8.2 Legitimate Power

Reciprocity, equity, and dependence. We have had to go beyond the legitimate power that comes from one's formal position and recognize other forms of legitimate power that may be more subtle, which draw on social norms such as (a) the legitimate power of reciprocity ('I did that for you, so you should feel obliged to do to this for me,' Gouldner, 1960), (b) equity ('I have worked hard and suffered, so I have a right to ask you to do something to make up for it,' Walster et al. 1978), and (c) responsibility or dependence, a norm saying that we have some obligation to help others who cannot help themselves and who are dependent upon us (Berkowitz and Daniels, 1963). (This form of legitimate power has sometimes been referred to as the 'power of the powerless.')

B. H. Raven, 1993

Legitimate power comes from someone who is willing to accept the others person's direction. It should be known that legitimate power is only effective if it is accepted by the person that it seeks to control. Being accepted by others who are not sought to be controlled will not help you gain power over the other person. This type of power is necessary within the organization as it aligns the goals with the direction of the company. The basis of legitimate power is spread from the top down to lower-level employees. Employees do tasks requested from those above them in the organization because they know it will benefit their organization. This is a use of legitimate power. Keep in mind the functional manager would have power over his or her staff some of whom are on the matrix manager's team so the matrix manager needs to work with the functional manager to effectively to leverage his or her support.

3.8.3 Expert Power and Referent Power

Positive and negative forms. Both of these bases of power were originally examined only in their positive forms: A subordinate may do what his or her supervisor asks because he or she feels that the supervisor knows best, or because the supervisor is someone admirable and desirable - who knows, the subordinate may aspire to be a supervisor someday. But it had been observed that sometimes we may do exactly the opposite of what the influencing agent does or desires that we do. Perhaps we recognize the expertise of the influencers, but distrust them and assume they are using their superior knowledge for their own best interests, not ours. Or perhaps we see the agent as someone whom we dislike, someone from whom we would prefer to distant from ourselves. Thus we incorporated into our system the concept of negative expert power and negative referent power.

B. H. Raven, 1993

Those who are perceived as experts by others in and outside the organization are said to have expert power. Most people seek and follow the advice of experts. Experts can be doctors, as well as athletic coaches, to name a few professions. Understand that most subordinates presume that executives know and understand each job in the organization. It should be known that in highly technical organizations subordinates may have more knowledge than management about aspects of a job. Executives may in fact be dependent on these individuals for their technical knowledge.

Project, program, and portfolio managers often have the skills and knowhow in the types of roles that are within programs they manage. They have worked their way up the ranks in their given field and often utilize this knowledge to get others to cooperate with them. These leaders can use this knowledge to get others to follow their plans and to lead them in day-to-day functions. For those leaders that do not have formal authority over their team this is a great option to seek power within the organization. It should be noted that it is beneficial to the project, program, or portfolio manager to have expert power. Cooperation and following orders will be more successful to those that have expert power when compared to those that do not. If you do not have expert power you can acquire this by becoming an expert in your domain though education. There are many avenues that you can explore depending on your situation and the level that you can commit to.

3.8.4 *Informational Power*

Direct and indirect. Informational power, or persuasion, is based on the information, or logical argument, that the influencing agent could present to the target in order to implement change. However, information can sometimes be more effective if it is presented indirectly. The early research on the effectiveness of 'overheard' communications, as compared to direct communications, would seem to bear this out. Falbo and Peplau (1980) found the direct/indirect dimension particularly important in their classification of power strategies. There is quite a difference between an influencing agent directly telling a target what s/he wants and why, vs. doing so through hints and suggestions. Johnson (1976) found that women were especially likely to use the indirect forms of information, men more likely to use direct information. Indirect information seems especially useful when a person in what is considered a low-power position attempts to influence someone in a superior position. Thus Stein (1971) notes that nurses who may feel that they have a useful suggestion in the treatment of a patient will tend to avoid direct informational influence, and will instead use an indirect approach such as 'This medication seemed helpful, doctor, for the patient down the hall who had a similar problem.' The more direct form of information (e.g., 'Doctor, this other medication, you must know, will be less likely to affect the patient's blood pressure, and would be much better, since he has a heart problem') might not only be less effective, but could result in disastrous interpersonal problems.

B. H. Raven, 1993

Informational power is when someone possesses the information needed and desired by others. This can work for and against the project, program, or portfolio manager. It is true that these roles hold much information about the work being performed but also rely on others for cooperation and ongoing sharing of information. A relationship where one person is always drawing information from another needs to find ways to make sharing information worthwhile and provide a "what's in it for me" to the other person. Once you find that person's currency you are on equal grounds and do not have to worry about the person terminating the relationship.

Now that you are familiar with the six bases of power within an organization, a thought-provoking point can be discussed. One of the challenges faced for the six bases of power is the scale of measurement for determining the following: employee satisfaction, job satisfaction and job performance. Understanding how each type of power draws conclusions for each area is vital knowledge for those seeking power over their followers and for working with others with various power bases in the organization. How will you measure effectiveness for your endeavors within the organization in regard to your team? Understanding what is asked of others and your goals is a good start in the process. You will have to reach out within the organization to several departments, mainly, human resources and functional managers, to find your answers in this area. Once you have your model determined you can proceed to utilize the sources of power. Remember once you have overstepped your power and authority it is hard to go back. Less is often more, and good judgment is a critical point in the process.

3.9 Understanding Expectations

When you work collaboratively in a matrix, knowing what is expected of you depends on the matrix type within the organization, which is vital to your success. Not knowing what others expect from you, or your expectations from others, leads to confusion, chaos, errors, and unsatisfactory results. According to the Project Management Institute (2013) if you work in a balanced or strong structure, you have moderate to high authority for your projects, programs, or portfolios respectively. In a weak matrix, you will have limited authority. In the case of a weak matrix structure the project manager is more of a coordinator or expediter. The expediter cannot directly make decisions and is a communications coordinator. He or she also cannot enforce decisions. The role of a project coordinator having more authority and reporting to a more senior manager can however make some decisions. How will you manage accordingly in these different situations? Will you have to adjust your management style accordingly? Will there be a conflict?

Coming up with a plan for your role will allow for greater flexibility in your approach to the situation. In a balanced matrix, you have mixed responsibility over the budget with the functional manager. In a strong matrix, the project, program, or portfolio manager has full responsibility over the budget, whereas in a weak matrix the functional manager has control over the budget. As you can see learning to collaborate and forge relationships will be in your favor.

Understanding the level of negotiating skills required should now be understood for your role. Learning how to effectively report upward in the organization often requires superior soft skills and tact.

Going beyond the basics, expectations means responsibility. The organization is trusts you to deliver results, often in challenging circumstances. Failing to deliver can mean the following: financial losses or loss of reputation. Building a reputation for delivering what is expected of you and not sacrificing power will greatly afford your future successes and opportunities within and outside of the organization.

3.10 Managerial Relationships

Working as a project, program, or portfolio manager you will interact more frequently and have more detailed conversations with other managers within the organization than your team members. If you want your work to get done smoothly, value these relationships sincerely. Managers have greater authority and the ability to do what members of your team cannot get done. From time to time you will rely on these individuals, from business-as-usual tasks to ones that need their support in the organization. Emphasizing cooperation and taking their needs into consideration is a good start to understanding managerial relationships. Sharing common goals and an understanding that you will go out of your way to be of assistance is only going to be beneficial when you need help and that person can assist you.

The goal of effective managerial relationships is to create partnerships rather than mere transactional relationships. This holds true to all relationships you will have in the organization not just with other managers. A transactional manager is not one that people look forward to seeing and working for on a regular basis. These relationships are hollow and lack the substance that makes them flourish. Resolving problems as a partnership is often easier and less time consuming, which means they are less costly to the organization as a whole. The leader that focuses on partnerships for the organization will be rewarded when it is time.

The advantages of forming partnerships is evident. Expanding your network, a second opinion on tough decisions, someone to "back you up" are a few of the many benefits. When you form a partnership you are putting yourself possibly in harm's way, you are relying on someone else. Forming a partnership that flourishes and meets both party's needs and goals takes time to form. This is not to say you have to wait a long time but recognize the dynamics that are in play when partnering up with someone else. Find someone that compliments your weaknesses and vice versa for you. Having a partnership where you get along grwelleat with the other person but they have little to offer in the form of subject matter expertise or another point of view will not be that effective for either you or the other person. It should go without saying that strong bonds and partnerships require constant upkeep. Never let a relationship sour or dull out because of the work that is piling in your desk.

3.11 Hidden Key Players in the Organization

Do you ever notice that there are nonmanagerial employees in your team that, because of either their role in the organization or their skill sets, are valued greater in the project, program, or portfolio manager's eye? These are hidden key players that are essential to your accomplishing your work. How should you approach these individuals? Should you praise them above others in your team? How can you acknowledge their contribution, without lessening the work of others? Recognizing the uniqueness of each team member builds healthy work environments and camaraderie among teams. A nonkey player today can become one tomorrow. Aligning your team members with such values through their contribution will produce better results. Therefore it is not advisable to overly celebrate those key people over everyone else. Strive to build each team member into a key player in the organization. This approach will only make your work stand out more and have a greater impact and wider reach than ever before.

3.12 Power Struggles

Project, program, and portfolio managers are inherently political roles. Working in a matrix does not lessen the political dynamics, but perhaps increases it. Balancing many relationships and commitments to a wide range of people all with their own pressing needs creates the environment for politics. A power struggle is where two or more people compete for influence. Fighting for your project for example, and needing several key resources while another leader also needs the resources at the same time is one that is commonplace. A rule of thumb is always fight for what is worth fighting for. Do not try to win all battles, but focus on those that are crucial for your work. As an example perhaps you can offset starting a particular phase of a project to when there is slack time and not fight for resources at the moment.

Always first spend the time to reconsider your position over the effort it takes to win each battle. Telling and showing the other person(s) that you made accommodations will work in your favor for the future when you are in this situation again but do not have slack time.

Perhaps in previous roles you worked in a different capacity within the organization or in another organization. Leveraging synergies from previous roles can allow for quicker turnaround time and being an expert that wears multiple hats in the organization. These advantages will come to play when you negotiate with others over influence that makeup power struggles.

3.13 Gatekeepers

A gatekeeper is someone who controls access to something or someone. Interfacing with gatekeepers in organizations is all too common for project, program, and portfolio managers. What is not always common or evident, however, is how to handle these communications and negotiations. Understanding expectations, etiquette and policies will make these experiences smoother and more successful for you. One of the most common tasks encountered with these individuals is schedules. Below is a four point plan to greatly reduce stress, errors and misunderstandings.

You should always include "duration" with every task to the gatekeeper. It is not enough to include the deadline for a task but include how long the task will take, the duration. When you have to adjust schedules quickly knowing the duration and having that number in front of you creates clarity. Understanding where there is or there is not slack for given tasks will be of great assistance to the gatekeeper and to you.

Be firm when you are creating and dealing with sign offs. Making changes is costly and often requires multiple people to adjust their schedules accordingly. Always obtain "official" sign offs that have the deadline written clearly before moving the next phase of your work. Be a person of integrity; deliver your commitments when you agreed upon in the first place. Managing expectations, schedule creation and maintenance are important of course, but being known for someone that is always delivering late will hurt you and your team's reputation. Your team could eventually hold beliefs that they are always late delivering results, so they will not push to ensure that this will not happen in the future, it will become business as usual.

Setting expectations at the start of the relationship with the gate-keeper will ensure later on that you can leverage these conversations, for example when the gatekeeper asks you to move up the deadline by three weeks. The project, program, and portfolio manager should be able to describe with ease the various parts of their work to the gate-keeper. They should be able to explain how long something will take and what resources are needed.

Having an individual that can play the good cop, bad cop scenario has many advantages. Perhaps unrealistic demands, or work that is out of the scope of the organization, or does not fit the organization's strategy is the problem. How do you handle these situations when they come up? Having someone in your team or organization that can partner with you and play the good cop or bad cop is necessary to provide a third party perspective to explain why an idea may not be a good one and to provide an alternative. This is not just common for project, program, and portfolio managers but for all job functions in the organization.

Finally, striving to plan for the worst and anticipate the best may not be the most optimistic of advice but it is true and tested. Anticipate that your contingency will actually happen. Are you pre-pared if it does? Do you need to take care of several tasks before-hand? Will it be your first time or have you done it before in the past? Knowing this will come in handy if the situations call for it. This lessens the stress and anxiety on you and your team. You will be implementing a plan rather than acting in chaos and perhaps confu-sion. Setting internal expectations that internal deadlines are just as important as client ones will ensure the work is completed at the best possible quality level.

3.14 DNA of the Organization

When you hear someone talk about its "secret sauce" they are often referring to the organization's DNA. What parts of the DNA directly touch the project, program, or portfolio manager? There is the organi-zational history, leadership influence, culture, values, and norms. This section will discuss how you can leverage your organization's DNA to deliver stellar results every time.

First, look at what information is or is not provided to you about your organization. Are there documents describing the history of the organization? What can be learned from them? How does your department fit in the big picture? Has it changed over the years? How have the core services and or products changed? How has your organization handled challenging times in the past? These data will provide an indication on its future. It is said that the past often predicts the future.

Dig deep about the backgrounds of the senior team of your organization. Why were they selected? Where were they in past roles? Were they from within the organization or outside from other firms? Does the organization believe in promoting from within? The senior leadership team is the heart beat of the organization. Do not just assume that the CEO is the only person you should know about. Does the senior leadership team have equal say in the organization? Knowing where influence lies will come into play when you need to get cooperation or tasks completed that require additional help from others.

There are four types of organizational cultures: clan, adhocracy, hierarchy and finally market. Knowing which one your organization is and what each type means will provide clarity and enable better communication channels with other departments.

A clan culture is a family in that they are focused on doing things together as a group and not individually. This culture values mentoring new and existing employees and are often nurturing in design. Adhocracy is one culture that is more entrepreneurial and focuses on risktaking to deliver results. As for market, this culture is result-oriented and has a strong focus on achievement and delivering results. Finally, there is the hierarchy culture, which is dominated by being structured and controlled. There are rewards for doing things right, and stability is valued.

It should be understood that there is in fact no correct or "better" organizational structure, they all promote some form of actions and frown upon others. Some cultures are better suited to rapid change, and others prefer a more methodical steady rhythm. The right culture is one that enables the organization to meet its goals and take it in the direction that is desired. Cultures can change over time; there is no rule that a clan culture cannot change into a hierarchy culture if the business requires it to do so to meet future goals and needs. It can now also be understood where the saying culture eats strategy for breakfast comes from. Having the need to implement a strategy often requires modification of or attention to the culture of the organization.

3.15 Common Organizational Functions

This section will describe the most common functions in an organization and how they affect and interact with the organizational structure. Perhaps you never looked at the various functions in your company in this matter and will take away a new appreciation for structure design. Following is a list of the most common functions for most organizations:

- CEO
- General Manager (GM)
- Operations
- Finance and Administration
- Marketing
- Engineering
- Product Manager

The CEO function is one of innovation, handling market changes, and keeping the team unified. This person is ultimately responsible for the short- and long-term strategy of the organization. The general manager or COO has autonomy from the CEO to produce results from the various verticals in the organization. The general manager is responsible for revenue streams and is held accountable by the CEO if goals are not met. It should be known that the general manager cannot provide approval for contracts or collect cash. This is the responsibility of the finance and administration department. The general manager requires the CEO's approval to alter the strategy of the organization. An effective CEO will not limit constructive criticism resulting in lessening the effectiveness of the organization. There is a healthy balance between effectiveness and efficiency for example.

To give some perspective, the general manager (GM) can be thought of as a mini CEO of his or her own business unit. There may be multiple general managers in the organization and they could be divided by regions such as Canada and Europe. They have sales and account managers underneath them, and their departments are where cash flows into the organization. GMs are responsible for acquiring new customers as well as meeting the needs of existing ones. Furthermore the GM has a budget and set targets for revenue that is expected to be brought into the organization.

Operations is an area role with a highly client-centric perspective and must produce results. Clients for operations can be either internal, external or a mix of both. The operations function needs to be stable and secure. Finance and administrative work must be performed without effort or they can quickly cause the organization to fail. The functions that make up finance and administration are human resources, legal and accounts payable/receivable. Marketing strategy is primarily about long-term innovation while constantly redefining and perfecting the vision. The engineering function is where efficient and effective designs are created and constructed to allow for operations to run their departments. Finally, there is product management where the various competing demands of the other groups in the organization are managed. Product managers have to drive high quality and profitability in the products they manage. Competing interests could be where operations want a stable product free of defects or bugs, while marketing wants one that is aligned with the long-range vision they have created.

The previous example is OK for a new product development but if it is a service organization then some modifications would have to be accordingly made. Service organizations experience drastic changes with the use of offshoring and information technology. Roles can be newly created or removed entirely from the corporate organizational chart. Focus on automation in recent years has excelled service availability and decreased costs. There has been much backlash from consumers and business customers alike on service levels decreasing as offshoring or automation takes place. Losing sight of the paying customer and the personal touch has been addressed in recent years. A new layer of customer service specialist roles have been created to ensure the customer does not fall through the cracks of the process.

3.16 Causes of Communications Breakdown

People are quick to place blame when there is a communication breakdown, but not all analyze in detail and find the root cause of the breakdown. There is a saying that goes, first seek to understand then be understood. What does that really mean and how can you apply it in the workplace? What are some key clues that your communication with someone may not be fully understood as you would like it to be? How can you help others communicate more effectively? These questions will be discussed in this section.

When you are trying to listen to someone, take notes on what the other person(s) is saying, ask for confirmation, and repeat the question back the way you understood it to ensure you first have it correctly if you are unsure at any point. If the first steps of communication are not met, it will be hard to have the back-and-forth pattern between people that leads to successful communication. How do you define successful communication? There can be a varied set of answers from different people depending on the topic, communication history and method of communication used. In selecting the communication method you should take all parties into consideration. What works best? What does not work for you and those you with whom you are communicating with? The savviest communicator will perform poorly if the wrong communication method is chosen. Technology in communication can be an enabler to some and the opposite to others who may not be comfortable or trained on the application or product. In fact, technology can magnify a problem if used or implemented incorrectly.

How can you know that your message is not being understood the way you want it to be received? People can be either asking too many questions or far too little, overlooking key points or continually discussing minor or nonissue topics. There could be some clues if they are looking at their cellphone or a clock frequently, leaving you with the impression that they are not fully engaged in the conversation. They could be short on details and defer to others to answer questions that they could answer. Being able to spot and troubleshoot communications is a key part of an overall communicating strategy. Overlooking this area will lead to poor results and dissatisfaction among everyone involved.

Having to communicate with someone who demonstrates poor communication skills on a regular basis is challenging to say the least. Taking initiative and working with the person to improve their skills and giving them the tools to succeed will benefit everyone involved and be worth the investment. Without listing the various ways someone can be a poor communicator, having a generic plan of action that you can use to quickly remedy the communication breakdown will appeal to everyone involved. First, document the communication. Ask the person to take notes since this forces them to participate and ask questions when they do not fully understand a topic being discussed. They will understand key points being made and by whom. Having a time keeper for the communication if it is a meeting will be helpful. Allow equal time between participants and start and end the meeting on time. Bringing an agreed-upon agenda to the meeting/discussion will not allow off-topic discussion and will focus on the agreed-upon topics for the meeting. Try to get to the root cause of the person's communication problems. Discuss in private if there is anything that you can do to help. Ask probing questions and take a sincere approach to improving their communication skill set.

This chapter has discussed how one can better understand his or her organizational structure. Without knowing the lay of the land, parts of the puzzle and how they interact, your current and future success will be greatly limited in a matrix organizational structure. Whether you have worked in a matrix structure before or this is your first time you should equally understand your organizational structure. Perhaps before reading this chapter you did not anticipate all the topics that have been discussed. They can bring up some questions. It is a good idea to meet and discuss your thoughts on the chapter with your professional group of six to ten people. You may find it interesting to hear their perspectives and gain another person's insight into the topic. Hearing others stories how they improved a colleague's communication skill set or how they interfaced with a gatekeeper in their past or present role will provide real world examples to solidify your knowledge on the topic. Try to use examples in the chapter in your meeting. For example, have someone play a person with poor communication skills and discuss as a group how to remedy this problem. The next chapter discusses ways to gain influence through volunteering in professional organizations for the project, program, and portfolio manager and focuses on understanding on how these volunteer opportunities can impact and influence one's career trajectory.

SUMMARY CHECKLIST

- Recognize how the organization structure and attributes effect the project, program, and portfolio manager.
- Be familiar with upward reporting and horizontal relationships.
- Recognize the five bases of power (expert, referent, reward, legitimate, and coercive).
- Discover the hidden key players of your team and nurture relationships with upcoming stars.
- Learn and understand what the DNA of your organization is and what its "secret sauce" is.
- Dig deeper and understand common causes of communication breakdowns in organizations.

4

GAINING INFLUENCE
THROUGH VOLUNTEERING

Looking back at Chapter 1 and the mind map of influential leaders you created, how do you currently stand with your identified skills for improvement, leadership traits, and your overall progress? This mind map will start each chapter to guide what this book discusses and to give you the opportunity to compare your goals and progress along your journey. Always have an open discussion with your group of six to ten professionals on where you stand and if you are having any roadblocks (Figure 4.1).

With 56% of survey respondents who work in a matrix environment (project, program, and portfolio managers) stating that volunteer roles inside the organization or outside such as with the Project Management Institute (PMI) have increased their ability to influence those in the organization, it is evident that this topic needs to be discussed further in detail. Remember there is a high association between influencing your organization and peers and your success rate in your role. This chapter discusses the practice of utilizing volunteer-based roles with the purpose to gain influence in and outside of your organization.

Volunteering is first to help others in need but can also be used to also benefit the volunteer. All good relationships should be mutually beneficial to all parties involved; having uneven balances in a relationship would cause dissatisfaction and limit the length of the relationship and how far it can grow. Knowing how to capitalize and create a win–win situation for the individual and the volunteer organization is the goal that this chapter aims to discuss. Perhaps you are doing great at your career but lack familiarity when dealing with people from multiple groups and divisions in the organization, as you do in a matrix structure, and it is limiting your success. Volunteering can bring new people into your activities and work that will create

Figure 4.1 Mind map of influential leaders.

the environment for improvement. This is just one example of the benefits of volunteering and how it can be used to acquire influence. Brainstorm (see Figure 4.2) with your professional group of six to ten individuals on what areas can you improve upon by using a mind map with your primary goal as the central topic.

We will continue with the example of improving your interactions when dealing with unfamiliar people and exploring your options. Recognizing your shortcomings and insecurities that you discussed with your group, write them down. When you look for a volunteer role seek one that touches upon what you want to work on even if is not the main focus of the role but still interests you. This gives you enough room to improve but not so much that it will make you uncomfortable being on the spot constantly. This example and others do not require you to volunteer in the sector that you work in during the day. Although this is common, volunteering in other industries can provide a fresh new perspective for you. Investigate PMI's Volunteer Management System and set up a profile that lists your areas of interest. Utilizing the volunteer website in addition to your local PMI chapter is a good starting point along with a local non-profit job board if you want to investigate opportunities in other spaces. There are virtual volunteer roles that may suit you better if you cannot commit to being at the same location regularly outside of your day job. PMI has a plethora of virtual and virtual + in person roles to choose from, which are updated on a regular basis.

Today's volunteers seek short engagements versus long-term commitments. They are self-directed, mobile, often have multiple interests,

Figure 4.2 Brainstorming.

and are driven by results. This may not surprise you when you compare these values and goals with the ones you have. Why volunteer in the first place? There are several valid reasons. First, you can learn a new skill; second, you will have the ability to develop leadership capacities; and third, you will network with new people. Limiting networking just to people in your industry cuts the effectiveness of networking to a minimum. Knowledge comes from a variety of sources, and you never know where a new relationship can lead you in the future. Perhaps you want to teach others a new skill or as discussed interact with new people on a regular basis. As you can see volunteering can greatly improve what you bring to the table in an organization and to the people around you. As touched upon there are a number of different types of volunteer roles that may interest you. These are in person or virtual roles or a combination of the two. Being in a virtual role means you do not work at the volunteer organizations facility, instead often doing the work at home or on a computer at any location during your free time. What suits you best? The following questions should assist you in answering this question. What are you trying to achieve? You would have discussed this with your group of six to ten professionals already. An important topic to discuss regarding volunteering is time commitment. How long and how often can you commit to volunteering? Would it make sense to commit once a week for two hours or can you do eight hours one day on the weekend? Shifting priorities come into play and knowing what level you can commit to before you start will make volunteering a more enjoyable experience.

How does your organization benefit from your volunteer activities? What can you expect to take back to the organization you work for after you have volunteered for several months? The answer to this question varies depending on the reason you want to volunteer, but some common answers are as follows: transferable skills, increased workplace commitment, reduced absenteeism, introduction of new knowledge into the workplace and better quality of work. You are investing in yourself while you are investing your own time for others. Speak to your manager prior to starting your volunteering and discuss if any accommodation needs to be made. It is always beneficial to have management from your organization support your improvement in endeavors and provide assistance when needed. Volunteering builds diversity among your group, provides greater links between the organization and the volunteer community. You may be surprised if your manager offers assistance in areas that you did not think of or use of resources within the organization.

A popular method of introducing new knowledge into the workplace is through lunch and learns. These are typically up to one hour in length and are presentations for promoting new knowledge to your team or another group in your organization. Some of the main topics of lunch and learns are skills training, professional development, product training, and personal development as well as life skills. Of course you can branch out from these topics depending on what you intend to present. The training in lunch and learns is less formal and less structured than other training you would receive in the workplace. Lunch and learns are not meant to teach subjects such as harassment in the workplace, and they promote satisfaction among the person doing the training and those who are attending the session.

During the tenure of your career so far, you may have sat in on some lunch and learns. Some probably were more beneficial to you than others, while others may have given you some ideas on making your own presentation at a session in the future. Try to focus the majority of your time presenting on a topic that will benefit the entire group. Focusing on a select few will not gain the benefits you want to see. Do an online survey prior to your presentation on proposed topics that you wish to present. A little planning and research goes a long way. Have any takeaways for the group already distributed before the end of the presentation. Provide contact information how people can follow up with any questions and of course ask for comments on the presentation! Try to create a buzz and snowball effect from your lunch and learn presentation. Take your ideas as far as you can get within your organization. Invite influencers from the organization as these people can magnify the desired results of the presentation.

There are several gaps that exist between volunteer organizations and the *modern* volunteer that will now be discussed. As mentioned, volunteers are looking for short-term commitments, while organizations are seeking long-term commitment. Volunteers are looking for group activities, but volunteer organizations are not always able to offer them. Volunteers seek to have the ability to create their own schedule and roles rather have these handed down from the volunteer organization. Although professionals come to volunteer organizations with skills, they often look to volunteer in tasks that are different from their day job. What advice can be given to the volunteer to best manage these gaps? The volunteer and the organization having the same goals and values will align them better. Spend time researching the volunteer organization and speak to current and past volunteers to get a better idea what you should expect from day one. Just as your manager at work should be accommodating you when possible, the volunteer organization should strive to accommodate your schedule. When both parties are accommodating to each other's needs the level of commitment increases.

How are you going to determine if you are achieving the goals that you set out prior to volunteering? Having a measurable system by which you can verify progress if is being made will only increase your velocity for continuous improvement. Have others help in measuring your success so as not to overlook any areas that you may not have thought of or forgotten. Your group of professionals that you meet with can be there to assist you for this process. You are forming long lasting partnerships with the volunteer organization and its members that go beyond what you are trying to achieve. All this hard work will pay off and then some!

4.1 How to Make a Meaningful Contribution

Joining a volunteer organization on any level and for any time period requires a certain commitment from you to that organization. Making a contribution of your time in a meaningful way that benefits others perhaps for years to come requires time. Just as in your role in your day job you need to put in maximum effort to get the results others are looking for and expecting. Be prepared for your volunteer role and ask beforehand if you need to bring any paperwork or materials. Following these rules and practices in your day job will make you more efficient as well as showing pride in your work, and others will be sure to take notice. You will create a name for yourself as someone that values other's time and wants to make meaningful changes and drive growth. Learning to be a self-sufficient leader is desirable. Take pride in the activities you do in your volunteer role and let them show though in your results. Volunteer-based organizations ask great things of their volunteers daily; your role is no exception. Being self-sufficient in your volunteer role translates into building your reputation as a leader in the organization for your day job. Colleagues and customers will come to you for help and advice and you will gain influence. Once you start making meaningful contributions you will find it is easier to make future contributions of a greater size and span.

4.2 Presentation Skills

Learning how to present better will get your message across to others in a more efficient, straightforward, and professional manner. You will have a higher chance of influencing those participating in your presentation. What do you think learning how to present better looks like to the presenter and the person sitting in the presentation? What makes up a good presentation? Think back to some presentations you were a part of that did a great job or not so great job and list out on a piece of paper what the differences were. We will now look into some key practices that you can implement to gain more influence.

In the age of smartphones and tablets those sitting in presentations are more easily distracted than ever before. Limit your presentation to short points and do not include lengthy paragraph style points. You can always provide supplementary information for those looking for the details. This builds into the next tip, know your audience. What type of presentation and format works best for them? Is there a certain time of day or day during the week that is better than others? This easy step will only ensure that those you wish to present to be most attentive and able to attend the presentation. Start on time, end on time. Practice your presentation to colleagues and see if they have any feedback. The order and selection of topics for the presentation dictate your message. A strong opening and conclusion of the necessary information will introduce and summarize your presentation to better reinforce the message. When you use figures select ones with the highest impact. Using the keep it simple rule try not to make it hard to understand and only have what is truly necessary. Again, provide any supplementary information packages for the details. Visual aids are a great way to display a complex topic or idea to others for the first time. With practice and presenting over time, you will not only be more efficient and effective, but your confidence in addressing people and dealing with difficult situations such as pushback will get easier over time. You will have more time to get your message across in shorter spans of time. In a matrix structure this skill is very valuable to the project, program or portfolio manager. Only a few of us are born public speakers. The majority of us get nervous, which in itself to a degree is not that bad. It will help you focus and manage your time and ideas that you are conveying to others to make the best impact.

4.3 Delegating Tasks

Volunteer-based organizations are people-oriented. They do a lot of the organization's work though their volunteers. As you can imagine there is a lot of delegating of tasks at all times as a result. Being a poor delegator shines through poorly in a volunteer organization with the work one has to accomplish. How can you be more effective and efficient as a volunteer when it comes to delegating tasks?

Have you worked with someone in the past that always met their goals working though others? Did you ever wonder what their secret was? Was it is a personality trait or something that can be learned? For the most part delegating can be learned though understanding the process, knowing what motivates others and being a team player. Understanding the process provides the roadmap for the task that is being asked of someone else. You need to understand in detail what you are asking someone to do. Is this the appropriate method? Is there a modified version that can be done? Does the person have the necessary knowledge, tools, and skills to do what is being asked? This is up to you to know. Often leaders work their way up the organization starting in roles where they themselves did the work and are familiar with what needs to be done.

Delegating tasks can be summarized by the acronym SMART: specific, measurable, agreed, realistic, time bound, ethical, and recorded. Think of a routine task that you have done in the past in your role and write the actions and events that make up the task. Have you followed the SMART acronym when asking a task of someone else? What was the result of the task? Were your objectives met? This may be something you can bring into your organization and volunteer organization for them to improve upon if you feel it would help.

4.4 Being a Leader

A leader is a coach and knows that a team that is easy to manage is not going as far as it can. When you think of what a leader looks like, you may look to business leaders, politicians, and religious leaders, but have you ever thought that everyone in your team can be a leader? Serving as a role model, being passionate, listening and communicating effectively, and having a positive attitude are all what makes up a leader. A team that is able to direct its own work to completion and help junior or senior members is worth its weight in gold. Not having formal authority over your team does not limit you to create this atmosphere when you have the ability to do so. Building lasting relationships with the team members' manager gives you the opportunity to have this manager continue your work when you are not working with the individual. By working collaboratively much progress can be made in a short period of time. The manager will be more than willing to take any suggestions knowing that you will work with him or her on an ongoing basis. Perhaps they are trying to modify the person's behavior or habits already, and two minds working together are better than one.

4.5 Being a Team Player

Being a team player sounds straightforward but it is a bit more complex than it may appear to some people. Being a team player does not mean simply going along with what the organization asks, but doing things that you would do not want to do on occasion and making the right decisions for the organization. It is serving for the greater cause, long after your employment with the organization is over. A team player always has his or her eyes open for quality issues, continuous improvement and lending a helping hand in another group or team whether one is asked or not. Perhaps you will be asked to share resources, meeting rooms, or equipment. It is your job to accommodate when possible. When you are perceived to be more cooperative, people will return the favor when you are in a bind.

4.6 Coaching Volunteers

Coaching others is something you are used to in your job in a matrix structure. You try to guide and influence those on your team to meet the needs of the project, program, and your portfolio. In a volunteer organization almost all of the volunteers have day jobs, and this is a secondary commitment. Recognizing that, you should emphasize the appreciation for the commitment they are making. Celebrating the small successes of individuals and teams will produce greater satisfaction and productivity.

4.7 Post Volunteering

So, assume you just ended your first volunteer position or it is coming to an end. You acquired a new skill, became a better leader and team player, and did some networking, but now what? How can you extend your volunteer role after it has ended? Your skill set has improved, and you became more marketable. Updating your resume and your LinkedIn profile while adding the contacts you made is a good first step. Nurturing relationships is one trait that successful networkers do that others may not consider. We discussed lunch and learns and how you can bring what you learned to your team.

The next chapter discusses how you go about to build, grow and maintain your coalition. In this chapter a strong case for volunteering has been made, as well you have begun to understand how making meaningful relationships with volunteers and volunteer organizations can create influence inside and outside your job. It is now time to take this discussion further and probe deeper into the topic.

Case Study

A select set of chapters in this book will have a case study concluding the chapter. The Chapter 4 "Gaining influence through Volunteering" case study will focus on the topics that you will interact with the most within the first 90 days in your role in a matrix structure. This will be the common theme for the case studies further in this book. Looking for answers to common problems and situations will let you manage more efficiently and effectively. Focusing on a select few topics discussed in this chapter will not only reinforce your knowledge but also apply practicality in seeing the topics in action. Case studies provide through analysis a greater level of learning and comprehension rather than only learning the framework of a topic.

This case study is going to look at JoAnn Trent and through examining the processes of volunteering decide if any gains were made for her career, and if so, what they were. Identifying the opportunity within an organization comes first. Volunteer roles differ slightly as there is more freedom in the particular role that you wish to work in so selecting the role then looking for the fit can not only take a lot longer but miss hidden roles that you might not have known about. JoAnn tried the obvious routes looking at a job boards and exploring other digital avenues such as LinkedIn and Twitter to exchange conversations with leaders in the sector she was looking to volunteer with. She got to know their current needs and where they are headed. For JoAnn it was going to her local PMI chapter, the Lakeshore Chapter in southern Ontario, and meeting current volunteers that she felt she fit in within the organization before she even applied for a role. JoAnn joined the marketing team as a coordinator.

Her commitments where to ensure the marketing sent out from the various teams met chapter guidelines and PMI standards. There were monthly in-person meetings where she got to present what she was working on. JoAnn quickly found herself to be at the hub of information regarding her team as a coordinator. Her current role was a project administrator in her full time job for a multinational retail chain. JoAnn worked in the finance department and did not think that she would ever get the opportunity to work in a marketing capacity. Her director at the PMI Lakeshore Chapter coached her initially on the job duties and process but JoAnn's knack for numbers and analytical thinking sped up the processes. JoAnn learned a creative side of herself that was not brought to light before. She took it on herself to present to the department directors at her workplace a more customer-focused way to market department guidelines and procedures. It was all too obvious to her that in her job the number one complaint was people not understanding the financial requirements of departments. The reason this was then possible to take place in her company was because she took a volunteer role in an area where she had limited experience and grew this into something special such that she could bring her new skills into her current full time role. JoAnn has since volunteered in three other roles within the PMI Lakeshore Chapter in communications and another in membership management.

CASE STUDY DISCUSSION QUESTIONS

- Have you had any positive experiences in volunteering to date that benefited your career?
- How can volunteering be associated to your career?
- Identify the opportunities that can be made by volunteering for your situation.
- What should organizations know about your volunteering job to help you in your career?

SUMMARY CHECKLIST

- Create a mind map of areas to improve through a volunteer role.
- Identify a volunteering organization and role.
- Determine time and location commitments.
- Make meaningful contribution when volunteering and do not forget to network.
- Create lunch and learn sessions for your organization.
- Post volunteering—follow-up, maintain contacts, and and celebrate successes.

5

BUILDING YOUR COALITION

Looking back at Chapter 1 and the mind map of influential leaders you created (see Figure 5.1), how do you currently stand with your identified skills for improvement, leadership traits and your overall progress? This mind map will start each chapter to guide what this book explains and to give you the opportunity to compare your goals and progress along your journey. Always have an open discussion with your group on where you stand and if you are have any roadblocks.

What is a coalition? Usually, a coalition is a union temporary in nature, but that can be a permanent agreement between two or more groups that seek to obtain more influence collectively than each individual group can obtain on its own. Recognizing its importance and the benefits forming coalitions can have, this chapter may be the place to break new grounds for you. Perhaps you have not read many documents or books that discuss the topic of building a coalition. There is no better time now that you are working in a matrix structure. Why does working in a matrix structure make this topic more valuable to you? Coalitions are the glue that will hold your community together, when there is friction or in difficult times. For reference, your community includes the following people: your team, clients, senior management, and any other people you interact with to do your job. Knowing how to acquire and gain allies, recruit others, grow and maintain your base, will undoubtedly increase the chances of your agenda being met. Figure 5.2 illustrates four main components of coalitions that were just discussed. Gaining allies helps you recruit others, which increases your base and the likelihood of the success of your agendas and projects. Each of these components has to be executed successfully in order to have a coalition. Neglecting any component and favoring others will cause unnecessary work on your behalf.

Looking for examples of coalitions can be as easy as reading the newspaper or turning on the television to a news network. Politics

Figure 5.1   Mind map of influential leaders.

are a well-tested example where coalitions take place. Some have said jokingly that the politician's campaign starts the first day after the last election. This is quite accurate and will ringtrue for you. Take a few minutes and think of some of the activities that politicians do on an ongoing basis. This book is not going to ask you to start a political career, but being able to put on your politician hat at work will be invaluable to your success in a matrix environment. Interfacing with people who have views and priorities different from which you or the team you represent will be common and routine. If you do not adapt yourself accordingly, you will undoubtedly suffer the losses and become frustrated over the "system" not being in your favor. Now we are going to discuss some key ways you can "work the system" in your favor, which will help with the projects, programs or portfolios that you manage.

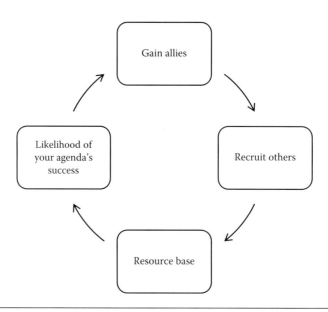

Figure 5.2   The four main components of coalitions.

What frustrates you on an ongoing basis working in a matrix structure? Perhaps people not taking your concerns as importantly as you do? How about your manager not being there to support you by providing resources for your projects, programs or portfolios? If you find that you are not getting cooperation when needed from certain people who you work with from other teams or groups then building a coalition will work in your favor. Do you have to debate with people and find yourself often at a loss on how to get your point across? Having others execute your mandate and the direction that you need to take makes your job easier and lets you focus on more important and pressing matters. Rest assured there are solutions to these problems.

5.1 Preparation and First Steps

Before you start to build your coalition always take the time to see if there are coalitions already in place in the organizational groups and teams where you want to build one (see Figure 5.3). What are the issues that are being focused upon? Is the coalition effective in its current form? If so, why and if not, why not? Do you notice any patterns? Can you find the history of the coalition? There is no sense reinventing the wheel, therefore, would forming a new coalition solve your problem or would making the existing one more effective achieve your goals? If you can collaborate with the existing coalition, there is a good chance of success as a lot of the initial work has been done already.

One of the first courses of actions would be to hold a brainstorming session. Look to get grass-root leaders and activists involved or people who can make a visible difference. Ask questions, such as the desired direction for the coalition and what would work well in the community. Write down your goals and the mission statement that you have created, these may seem to be minor points but are important to ensure everyone is in agreement and on the same page. When you document your meetings it formalizes the conversations and does not

Figure 5.3 Preparation and first steps.

leave room for misinterpretation. These are the documents people will refer to at a later date if there is a disagreement or misunderstanding.

The next step is to hand out responsibilities to the members. You need to determine whether the structure is to be leaderless, collective, or have one leader. What will work best to achieve your goals and the coalition's goals? Everyone has to win when it comes to coalitions. One person cannot take and not give; there must be balance among the coalition members. How often and where should the coalition meet? Try to compromise to meet the needs of the majority of the coalition members, do not let the loud voice of the few overtake the majority. Is the commitment that is being asked realistic for all its members? These initial steps have lasting impact on the effectiveness and efficiency of your coalition. Taking the proper time will allow time for your coalition to meet your needs for the long term.

5.2 How to Be a Politician

If you were to draw a pie chart what would be the percentages and names of one of the activities that you feel a successful politician would need to have? Discuss with your support group to get a more collective view on the topic. Being a successful politician can be summed up in the following five key steps:

1. Understand your community.
2. Practice your public speaking and make lasting connections with a variety of people in your community.
3. Keep up with current events and understand the history of your community.
4. Find one or two closely related politicians or leaders who have successfully done what you want to achieve and study them.
5. Start small and constantly challenge yourself to grow.

An examination of each key step follows.

5.2.1 Understand Your Community

Your community is all-inclusive group of people; it should not single out individuals or favor a few. Appealing to the majority requires a fine balancing act of tact and diplomacy from yourself. This may be challenging to learn if you never needed to use these skills in your professional life. As it has been said before in this book, success will come with practice and perseverance. Winning over others does not require bribery or favors for cooperation. When it comes down to it, meeting the needs of the people for today and the future will bring everyone together. If you offered special favors, kickbacks, or bribes you always have to maintain those acts, often with greater value over time. It is a slippery slope indeed and a position you should avoid. Try to on a semiregular basis survey your community to make sure you are aware of any new needs or demands. You can have all the data at your hands, but if they are not accurate or you do not act upon the data, people will not think there is value in collecting the data. In fact, incorrect data or making decisions on wrong points is just as harmful as not having any information in the first place.

5.2.2 Public Speaking

Chapter 2 discussed joining a local Toastmasters group to improve your public speaking. It will be suggested again that public speaking has to be practiced to be improved. Almost every successful global influencer worked to improve his or her public speaking. These influencers got to their level of proficiency though practice and working on their weaknesses and focusing on their strengths. As an alternative, if Toastmasters is not available to you speak in front of your support group. Even though you are comfortable with them, and they are not strangers, when you make a speech you are put on the spot and have to perform. You will still get nervous and need to work at practicing your gestures, for example. Over time you will improve and be able to tackle more adventurous and important speaking engagements. Connecting with your audience is a skill that can be learned by those that put in the effort and time.

5.2.3 Current Events

This step may come easily to some while others will have to work at it. Some people naturally soak up the global, national and local current events scene. They are drawn to keeping abreast of "the issue of today," while others naturally shy away from current events and are not as vocal as others on this topic. If you fall into the latter, try the following. Watch a 24-hour news channel and start to learn the events that are being discussed. Try to memorize key points and players. This will provide you with the training ground when you talk to members of your coalition. Learning their issues and events that happen within the coalition is at the heart of what makes them take on certain issues and form and shape their views.

5.2.4 Look for a Political Mentor

Mentors help you set career goals and introduce you to professional resources that were not known before. These are just some of the uses of having a mentor. This book suggests having a few political mentors that you look up to and can learn from. This step should not be all that challenging and take much time but will provide assistance and direction to you. It is going to be asked that you search for political mentors and take this step with your support group to get a greater range of responses. More than likely you have one or two political mentors in mind, but it is going to be asked that you choose three with at least one that your group picks for you. Your support group knows your goals and the journey you have undertaken, it is also likely they know what you need to achieve your goal and be successful in a matrix environment.

This book is going to ask that you spend 15 to 20 minutes every day reading about your political mentors. Try not to focus on the same sort of information but take at a 360° look at their political life.

5.2.5 Humble Beginnings

You may tackle tremendous goals in your professional life; this book suggests gradually building towards your ultimate goal in a steady manner though mastery of your skills. Do not go to the next step until you master the existing step. Every action and step this book discusses and talks about has meaning and importance to you in your project, program or portfolio management career. Each step deserves to be mastered and understood fully. This approach is going to give you great value and the foundation to grow upon in your career. Just as you would not want to be in a racing car that was rushed to be assembled, you do not want to rush your professional development. Aim to go at a speed which will not trip you up over yourself and which you can maintain for the long run, but is not so slow as to be n inefficient for yourself or your team.

5.3 The Three Resources in Politics

There are three competing resource types that you will encounter in politics. Maintaining a balance is more of an art then a science. Through experience and acquiring knowledge you can improve your understanding of how one interacts with another, as well as what works for your coalition. The three resources needed by politics are

- *Money:* The cost in currency to accomplish a task or goal.
- *Time:* This is the time between the present and the election vote.
- *People:* The members, volunteers, and leaders needed to implement a plan.

These three resources should sound familiar to what is needed in your job in project, program, or portfolio management, so you have some idea of how to utilize these resources in an efficient and effective manner.

Effective communication skills and being able to persuade others takes practice to develop.

There has been discussion on joining a local Toastmasters group to improve your public speaking, but we are going to discuss the following five must-have skills for success in your coalition:

1. Find common ground between yourself and the people you are communicating with regularly to form the base of your relationship.
2. First seek to understand the other person, then seek to be understood. Often someone tries to interrupt the other before they are done speaking.
3. Give a genuine impression that you both are on the same team.
4. Summarize what the person said before you offer a comment so the person knows you understand his or her points of view and were listening.
5. Always extend the olive branch of peace when there is disagreement or if the person feels hurt by what was said or done.

These skills can be improved though mock scenarios with your support group. Spend up to one session working on them.

5.4 Coalition Stalemates

A stalemate is when there is no immediate or foreseeable action that can be taken to make progress on an issue or action. Stalemates are all too much a reality and more common than you think in coalitions, but there are solutions that can take place to remedy the problem. Having common ground and goals with all parties of the coalition comes in particularly handy for stalemate situations. These common goals should be discussed in the first meeting with the individuals. Try to look at past events where all parties met at least half way and did not draw a line in the sand on positions or topics. You will be amazed how productive you can be when no one has a hidden agenda. If you do however run into someone with his or her own agenda, which is common, and this agenda does not support your topics or goals, and you feel it is not important, you need to emphasize that cooperation among the group will allow for future progress. Find what is truly important to them and say that if the person does not cooperate you may not be able to support or help them in the future. Once you find someone's currency, which is especially important, you have a greater chance of getting buy-in and long-term support. It is not about winning the battle; it is about winning the war. It is far too often that someone permanently damages the relationship over nonessential topics. Even the best relationship requires tact and diplomacy; do not undermine this subtle though but important point.

5.5 Levels of Participation within a Coalition

At what level can the members of your coalition effectively participate? Never assume you know even if you have some background on the members. There are two levels that are going to be discussed that one can participate: working together and agreeing not to compete and sharing resources. There is a good chance that these terms are new to you so this book will now provide some background on each level.

5.5.1 Working Together and Agreeing Not to Compete

Working together implies sharing tasks and the workload on a topic or issue. It does not however automatically imply a 50–50 division of labor. This can be sorted out among the coalition members but has to be for the good of all parties inclusive. Specifically, when you agree not to compete you are saying that in good faith you will respect where the line has been drawn, and everyone has agreed upon to act in good faith not to cross that line. There should be some safeguards in place so accidents or misunderstandings no matter how they were caused do not impact your agreement. Do not let the misunderstandings of today wreck the progress and successes of tomorrow.

5.5.2 Share Resources

Just as in working together and agreeing not to compete, it does not imply that a 50–50 division of resources are to be shared. All parties however must agree to the distribution of resources in order to have a meaningful coalition and lasting relationship. Sharing resources could mean office space, personnel, equipment or whatever else is asked from the various members of the coalition.

5.6 Challenges Faced in Coalitions

This chapter has already brought up some potential challenges that can be faced in a coalition. More details will follow. The more you understand about what can go astray; you have a better opportunity to stop it from happening or can lessen its effect if it does happen for your coalition. There is no better time to discuss this generally with your support group and then discuss the challenges that can be faced in your unique situation.

5.6.1 Coalition Focus

Common values that all parties can agree upon, perhaps already in practice, will stand a better chance than ones that are radical and new for each member of the coalition. Discuss how things were done successfully prior to forming a coalition. Try to incorporate the best practices from each group while recognizing the new single entity.

What others have done well and where they have perhaps failed in the past can all be a lesson on the focus the coalition should be headed towards now and in the future.

5.6.2 Member Motivation

Motivation is independent of coalition size, complexity, and resources shared. Are members willing to speak as one? Can members clearly articulate what they want to others and negotiate fairly though establishing trust among each other? Depending on the members' motivation, their tactics and objectives become clear to others. For example wanting to understand how your issues fit into the broader network of the coalition's issues can show others you see merit in their concerns. Spotting and dealing with someone quickly that acts independently to your coalition can keep groups on track. Having a formal or perhaps informal process to penalize someone that goes against the group's goals, missions, and strategic plan can keep the coalition successful and fruitful in nature. The saying it only takes a few rotten apples to ruin the bunch stands true for coalitions. It should be noted that if someone that feels his or her voice is not being heard or if a perceived unfair act happens, this should be dealt with outside of the process to deal with those that jeopardize the coalition.

5.6.3 Decision Making

Instinctively we make decisions that would improve our position or get something we want. What is going to be asked in a coalition is thinking of the groups and members of the coalition before your personal interest. This can be challenging and requires discipline and a genuine interest in seeking an agreement with the coalition. Often there can be conflicts of interest in the desired outcomes and goals that want to be achieved. Being able to work though these hurdles is difficult even for the most cooperative individual. Look to make concrete goals together that are manageable. It may be positive to have long-term goals but strive for the mid-term when setting goals among coalition members. This decreases the potential of long-term conflicts while you are working on your mid-term goals. Strategizing and planning at the onset of the coalition forming and operating will greatly increase the collective success that will be made. Having patience as discussed in previous chapters will work in your favor even though it may appear to slow down the progress that you and others want to make.

5.6.4 Weak Links and Sharing Trust

How do you handle sensitive issues such as dealing with weak links and sharing trust in coalitions? It has already been said that creating safeguards for your coalition will only preserve its integrity and keep it aligned in its strategic direction. Some people trust one another from the onset of a relationship, while others require some time to get to the same level. This level of trust cannot always happen at the start of your coalition and requires building over time. Learning how people reason with their ideas and takee into consideration that the views of others do not come on day one. This can more often than not be a sure way to fail and lose trust in others. Though trust building activities the coalition can be where it should be within a reasonable time frame.

When you are faced with a weak link in your coalition your guard will be up, and your interactions will be shorter and more to the point as in a transactional relationship. Give the other person the opportunity to gain your trust and that of others though calculated situations where the risk is not that great. Having a safety net if they do not cooperate will lessen the chance that in the future you will be hesitant to try again. Always have the door open for negotiating and invite these individuals to be in your inner circle of coalition members. This can be what may make the person(s) a stronger link for your coalition. Perhaps they had difficulties in the past in trusting others and are the way they are now because of it. Never assume you know the full story as often there are pieces of information that are unknown or not communicated correctly. Human interactions are complex; making them into simple terms will remove the depth and the details, which are the parts you need to know to make good, informed decisions on people and topics for your coalition.

5.7 Typical Problems for Many Coalitions

As discussed, there are some common problems that you will run into during the life cycle of your coalition. Knowing how to spot and recognize these common problems will save you and the coalition members the stress, time, and often money that it takes to work through and solve these common problems. As discussed already, trust, integrity, and common goals are among the cornerstones for building relationships, which is at the heart what a coalition is. This book will now go beyond these problems and discuss more complex and lengthy situations that can arise. It is a good idea after reading this section to discuss with your support team if they have any other common problems that you may run into in your own unique situation.

A coalition has to operate like a well-oiled machine to meet its members' collective and unique goals. Once you are able to break down some functional parts of a coalition, you can assign key member(s) to the various responsibilities. These functional parts are as follows: leadership capability, adaptive capability, management capability, technical capability, and cultural capability. How will you fill each functional part in your coalition? Will individuals have multiple roles, or will there be shared responsibilities among several members? Discussing each member's strength and experiences will initially fill several roles but do also consider your coalition's goals. Do the individuals fit in with your goals? Do you foresee conflicts or overreach in power? Discuss as a group and if necessary vote accordingly to fill these roles. Voting serves a good purpose in a coalition. Each member gets a fair share at making decisions, and a few members cannot overtake the group and change its direction without the consent of the majority of the coalition. There should be a process that in the event of a tie a decision can be made. Come up with what you agree upon and put your coalition plan documents in writing in.

5.8 Attributes and Achievements of Successful Coalitions

Successful coalitions, much like families, have roles for its members and a hierarchy within them. This hierarchy is designed with a purpose and its use has withstood the test of time. It is comparable to a family unit that can survive and meet its established goals. In a coalition, for example, there should be someone to go to for counsel in issues and someone to hand out punishment if the need arises. Picking members of your coalition based on needs that go beyond your goal should be taken into consideration. How will each member interact with others and how close to their potential can this interaction reach? Just taking a minute to think in this way will bring up a series of questions that need to be answered. Placing someone in your coalition is just the same as in your organization and requires soft skills and a level of experience. If you lack these skills and are more technically inclined, look into having a partner that shares your goals and vision on an equal playing field to lead the coalition. Vice-versa if you have the soft skills and lack the technical skill set seek a partner that has the technical skills to compliment you. There are benefits of partnerships, and there are also some benefits of taking it on your own. Which makes the most sense for you? Successful coalitions are built though strategically thinking and planning, and there is no more important area than those people who you will be working side by side with on a regular basis.

Just as important as finding the right individuals when there is someone that does not fit the coalition's values, goals or risks the future of the coalition, a process ideally should be in place to remove this person. No person should be that valuable that they can reduce the effectiveness of the coalition and stay on as a member. The need for one person in a coalition decreases that persons effectiveness overall for the group as they can only focus on so many areas at one time and are needed everywhere. Some leaders have a hard time passing up someone that has the technical skill set but lacks skills in other areas that cause the disturbance. It may take time to replace that individual but the long-term success will remain intact, and the ability to focus time on the coalitions defined goals and mission makes up for the loss. Never let short-term plans hinder long-term success and goals.

5.9 How to Effectively Host a Meeting with a Coalition

It goes without question that you will have a number of different types of meetings within your coalition's lifespan. These types of meetings are as follows: ad-hoc, in-person, and remote. This section discusses how you can maximize your and others' effectiveness when hosting a meeting. There are commonalities for each meeting: punctuality, diplomacy, roles, and respect. Meetings are to start on time and end on time. Having respect for the meeting members will ensure cooperation for future meetings and ensure the meeting agenda was met. The basic roles for meetings are to have a meeting organizer, leader, scribe, and time keeper. There may be other roles depending on meeting size, topic, and complexity, but these will always have a place for you in your coalition. Take time to find out the right person for each role for your meetings.

Ad-hoc meetings happen with little or no notice. They could be to discuss a hot topic or how to handle a situation that requires immediate attention. They are often shorter and less formal then in-person or remote meetings. There often are fewer people at these meetings, perhaps only a few key stakeholders or a small team. Each meeting type has a specific purpose, and when you misuse the type for the proper solution you lessen the effectiveness and cause great inefficiencies for the people involved and the agenda that is to be discussed. If you are unsure if a full meeting is needed or if an ad-hoc one is the best approach, try to keep the rule of five in hand. There should be no more than five members and five topics in the ad-hoc meeting. If this is not the case, you need to organize a full meeting to give adequate consideration to the topics and people involved. The more people and topics you add the more complex it gets and more time is required to discuss the agenda respectfully. Do not let the name fool you: ad-hoc meetings require a scribe to take meeting minutes and of course a leader and time keeper. Keeping proper administration duties for meetings will allow for fast retrieval of past meeting action items and meeting minutes when the need arises, and it will. Never be caught without the full details in your hand when the occasion arises.

In-person and remote meetings are formal, structured, and of longer duration than ad-hoc meetings. This is the appropriate place to discuss topics that require moderate to lengthy debate and consensus among a greater number of meeting attendees. This does not mean everything can be discussed in one meeting. Perhaps a few meetings are required depending on the nature of the topic, complexity, and people involved.

What makes a meeting a success is having the ability to change your mind if someone presents a compelling argument to do so. Working in the interest of the group and not in your own interests, not stalling, blaming, or attacking others while trying to prove your point are best practices. Coming prepared means being up to date on the agenda and any discussions that require your input. Achieving this list although long is more than doable. It does require a sustained effort not only on your part but on the part of other meeting attendees as well.

5.10 Mitigating Disagreements

> Not all coalitional behaviors may appear to be beneficial in achieving
> the common good.
>
> **Dupont, C., 1996, p. 61**

This quote is valid and must be understood so that your coalition does not fall short of everyone's expectations and desired outcomes. When you disagree are you disagreeing with the idea or the person who has the idea? Separating the parts of an argument and being able to rationalize what has been said is the way that you will come to an agreement on the topic and can move forward. Perhaps the person(s) was not cooperating in the past, and you let that past discussion taint your current decision. It is often done, and without much valid cause people tend to keep a running tally of who wronged them in the past and feel if they do not cooperate in future discussions it is a way to get back at the individual(s). There is not a winners' circle for those who use revenge and tactics that are not for the good of the group. Leadership as discussed in previous chapters is about taking responsibility and that translates into doing what is right, not what is easy or comfortable to do. Be the person that changes the atmosphere in which decisions are made, and others will follow suit. It does not need saying twice that everyone at the end of the day wants to see progress; those that do not fail to make a transition to being a leader in a given situation.

The following quote from Dupont (1996) discusses how the better handle disagreements within your coalition when they arise. Perhaps you just had to handle disagreements with one or two people at most in the past. Your plan of action and what is required of you to solve these disagreements are now different in nature.

> Cooperative negotiations can be viewed in terms of action-oriented coalitions working toward a mutually acceptable outcome, essentially through persuasion and influence. Competitive negotiations can be seen from the perspective of confrontational coalitions involved in a search for a minimally acceptable outcome that can be achieved by competitive more than by consensual strategies. Coalition members may achieve short-term gains. The way a coalition operates bears a close resemblance

to the way an actor in a dyadic or multilateral negotiation manages to identify the salient points in the agenda, explores and tests the opponents' interests and behaviors, exerts influence or pressure, and adjusts positions to induce or force agreement. Minority coalitions often act to achieve goals on certain substantive issues and to negotiate the contents of proposed formulas and details of agreements inspired by the majority, the 'winning' coalitions. Their means can involve foot dragging, systematic use of objections, recourse to precedents or norms, insistence on repeated redrafting, and threats of impasses and breakdown.

Dupont, C., 1996, pp. 60–61

The goal of this chapter is to show how you can better build and utilize the coalition that you formed or joined. This chapter suggests and recommends understanding how to be a politician and the roles and duties that this encompasses. With limited or no authority over your team, you need to form coalitions with key members of various groups inside and outside your organization. This chapter sheds light on how coalitions operate and the soft skills and tact that are needed to have a successful one. The next chapter discusses how to gain influence over others that you have limited to no formal authority over in your work.

Case Study

Sharon Scotch was tasked with implementing a pilot CRM program within a 2500 person organization. Her background is in business analysis, and this would be her first project as a project manager. The organizational maturity level was very low and the challenge was understood at the onset of the project when signing the project charter. Plagued with political challenges and pitfalls Sharon was eager to take on this new role and responsibility. What she knew first was that before anything happened she needed to form a coalition in the organization of the various groups involved or nothing would ever get done or signed off. Sharon had only worked for the organization for five months and knew a little about how "things get done" in the company. Her first coalition member was the CIO in her department as he had skin in the game for her project so would be a quick win and enable her to get others on board with little effort.

The concerns that the CIO addressed were valued and helped Sharon understand the challenges that were faced within the coalition at her company. Finding individuals that fit in with her goals was key, not the number count of people in the room. Sharon eventually met with five key business leaders in various groups in the organization. Sharon ran into numerous challenges such as not having enough license for all users and having to have administrative assistants access the CRM on behalf of the requested user seeing that this was a pilot. Sharon was lucky that there were not too many showdowns or people limiting access to the resources she required. Through diplomacy, tact, and her business analyst background, she was able to capture all requirements up front, which saved her project.

Sharon created a lessons-learned document though a workshop of key players in the organization. She listened to their concerns and when it came time to run the full rollout she was selected as the project manager. The coalition meets biweekly and discusses any challenges and opportunities that need to be addressed. It is a multi-cosmopolitan group of individuals that range from junior analysts to C-level executives.

Sharon greatly expanded her knowledge on public speaking, delegating, and presenting new topics to senior leaders who may have had their own agenda already in place before meeting Sharon.

Sharon took it on herself to go to five Toastmaster meetings where she practiced the key presentations for her CRM project. She was coached by fellow toastmasters on how to sell an idea or concept verbally. She since has gone back for every other significant presentation as a sounding board prior to speaking.

CASE STUDY DISCUSSION QUESTIONS

- What is the opportunity in that Sharon was presented with?
- Why did others contribute to Sharon's success?
- Are there any noneconomic risks?
- What kind of follow-up should Sharon make to her success?

SUMMARY CHECKLIST

- Recognize the main components of a coalition.
- How will you be a politician in your role?
- Find your political mentor.
- Recognize the levels of participation within a coalition.
- Explain differences between ad-hoc, in-person, and remote meetings.

6

GAINING INFLUENCE

Looking back at Chapter 1 and the mind map of influential leaders you created (see Figure 6.1), how do you currently stand with your identified skills for improvement, leadership traits, and your overall progress? This mind map will start each chapter to guide what this book teaches and to give you the opportunity to compare your goals and progress along your journey. Always have an open discussion with your group on where you stand and whether you have any roadblocks.

6.1 Defining Your Goals and Priorities

What is your reason for wanting to gain influence over your colleagues? Do you need to buy in on a particular initiative that you are leading? Chances are there are multiple goals that you have, but this list must be prioritized in order to be effective and not stretch your resources. A simple prioritization is listing your time constraints and the potential benefits in order. Aim for the low-hanging fruit first and tackle larger goals that are more complex afterward. Building momentum will enable you to tackle these more complex goals when you run into challenges (and you more than likely will). Perhaps, the people you worked with in your first few initiatives can be of assistance. Never assume everyone you interact with can be of assistance to you in some way; some will want to help, while others may not, and some may surprise you and even volunteer. When you realize this lesson, you are effectively lessening the burden on yourself and freeing up some time and energy that can be used elsewhere. Many tradeoffs are made when gaining influence over others. There is never a situation where you have to do something or else you lose. There is always room to reasses both parties' wants, needs, goals, and renegotiate. Most people listen to reason, and if you can tell them a compelling story why they should cooperate, chances are they will. This chapter will explain the "what is in it for me" and "why should I listen to you

Figure 6.1   Mind map of influential leaders.

when I think I know more on the topic or issue." Negotiating happens in everyday life, which to a degree you have learned to master. In the workplace just as in other settings the person who is most prepared, able to reason with others, and can demonstrate taking your interests in the issue at hand will be successful.

Before we get started further in this chapter, take the next 15 minutes or so and think of past situations where you had to negotiate and were either successful or not. Write down what you believe to be the root cause of success or failure. Learning from the past will enable you to be successful in the future. Following are some common success factors for negotiating with others:

- Acquire as much information as you can before making key decisions
- Postpone unclear directives from others and look to negotiate common areas first
- Reveal your position only if you have to in order to get buy-in
- Never negotiate when there is little time on hand

Compare this list to the one you just made and see how many similarities match your list. Although this approach is not going to determine your overall success, it can show if you are starting in the right direction. If the comparison is quite different, discuss with your support team and try to understand what caused these differences. Perhaps you were in a unique situation, but there should be some similarities. When you negotiate with an individual or group(s) and you want their lasting cooperation, not just initial agreement, there must be a compelling reason for them to do so. Being deceitful or withholding information perhaps can get a "yes," but this "yes" will not translate into long-term fruitful commitment by all parties. This method to obtain a long-term commitment requires much more work and creativity on your part, but it is the only way to align everyone and get the cooperation you need right now.

6.1.1 Getting Others Onboard with Your Agenda

Getting others onboard with your agenda really means aligning priorities and goals with their support and buy in with the topic or agenda on hand. Think for a minute, do you think it is possible to get cooperation but not have someone buy-in to your agenda? It sure is. Perhaps the person(s) whom you are working with are being forced to cooperate but do not have the resources or have other priorities outside what you have outlined. How successful would this venture be? Not very, unfortunately this happens more often than people want to admit. Everything starts at the onset of the relationship and builds from there. The sooner you reach across the aisle and agree that your goals are also my goals, the sooner you can make progress with your agenda. You now know there will be hurdles to overcome and that swift action on your part keeps progress happening and maintaining momentum, which is very important to deter others from stalling and introducing roadblocks in your agenda. Once one person starts stalling and not cooperating others may join in or be asked to join in by the individual(s) who is causing progress to be halted. Getting buy-in is like changing the direction of the *Titanic:* it is often a slow process but once realigned it is equally hard to change its new direction. This is why such an emphasis is being placed upon the initial few conversations with those you wish to influence. Perhaps there will not be many chances to meet and regroup and that your first three meetings will dictate the course of influence you will have over others.

It is noteworthy to mention that you may be asked to take someone's place that was mid-way in negotiating and need to get cooperation. That is you did not start from the beginning and there is mending to the relationship that is needed. You could also be the new person on the block and you need to prove yourself to your team and those that you need influence with. Having credibility in past roles and within the organization will go a long way to demonstrating to others that you are the right person to take on the agenda. This is often a reality for many project, program, and portfolio managers. When they start a new job often, they are taking on work that is already in progress. Relationships need to be established, and trust has to be created with stakeholders, management, and colleagues. This buy-in not only is for the work that is being performed but for the success of the individual in the role itself.

6.2 Becoming Strategic

When you think of "being strategic," what comes to mind? The following words and phrases commonly come up on the topic: managing change, juggling priorities, leadership, setting goals, and quick thinking. What some people forget and leave out is the people aspect in strategy. No strategy can be realized if the people working on it cause it to do so. The first step of being strategic should come easy as this book has been emphasizing the soft skills, which often cause a smooth or difficult time with the intended strategy. What is now going to be discussed are the common elements that are in successful strategies as well as Michael Porter's advancement of the SWOT (Strengths, Weaknesses, Opportunities, Threats) tool and its application specific for your role. Understanding what SWOT is and where it came from will also be discussed.

This book is going to compare and contrast you, the project, program, or portfolio manager to a business. As a result, you will look at your role in a new light, and the outcome will be that you will react differently when presented with a situation that requires you to be influential and gain influence over others. Figure 6.2 illustrates the competitive scope as well as the source of competitive advantage. We will look at the source of competitive advantage first. There are two paths that you can take, low cost or differentiation as a source of competitive advantage. How this translates into actionable items for

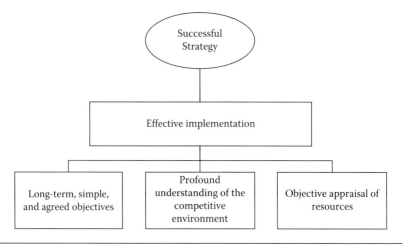

Figure 6.2 Common elements in successful strategies. (From Grant, R., *Contemporary Strategy Analysis* (5th edn.), Blackwell Publishing, Malden, MA, 2005, p. 7, Figure 1.1. With permission.)

you are that you can either undertake an agenda that has low cost to your resources, or you can seek to differentiate in multiple directions. Figure 6.3 shows how this strategy is organized in Porters Generic Strategies (Grant, 2005, p. 243, Figure 7.5). There are situations that call for either strategy and knowing which one to apply will save you time and help you reach your goals sooner and with less energy spent on the efforts. If you are looking at targeting a specific segment of individuals then you want to focus, and if you are looking at a large dispersed group then you are going to look into one of being low cost of differentiating yourself if it fits into your overall strategy.

When you think of low cost you may think of inexpensive or poor quality and not meeting your needs. This is not always true. Low cost for this book means looking for low-hanging fruit and quick wins. You are trying to maximize all available resources in order to gain influence as you are targeting a wide and dispersed audience base. However, if you need to have multiple strategies going on at the same time for various reasons to gain influence over a large group of individuals, then you may want to differentiate you positions. How this can play out, for example, is you need to target various levels of seniority or age groups within the organization to influence. In this case, it makes sense to differentiate to the various individuals. The one caveat is that differentiation takes up more resources and can cost more of your time and capital to acquire influence. Overspending your competitive advantage and not choosing the right option based on your goals and objectives will only put you further behind and position yourself with less of a chance to influence those that you desire.

Thinking strategically has been discussed and now with this example and with this lesson you can see how the strategies you use enable

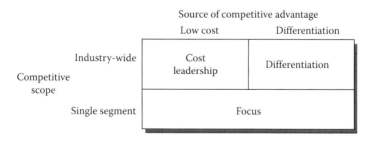

Figure 6.3 Porters generic strategies. (From Grant, R., *Contemporary Strategy Analysis* (5th edn.), Blackwell Publishing, Malden, MA, 2005, p. 243, Figure 7.5. With permission.)

or restrict your ability to influence key players. Look back and think how you may have applied this knowledge in your past positions. It does not take much to recognize that having a strategy and positioning yourself can greatly increase the level of success you will have now and in the future in a matrix structure.

6.3 Ethics in Influencing Others

Ethics play a substantial role for you, particularly within a matrix structure. Sticking to your commitments and your obligations to others will enable you to build trust and grow relationships. Relationships, as discussed, are one of the key components that make for a successful project within this structure type. If a colleague or coworker feels that you do not have their interest in hand they will not commit to you and live your vision, and in turn this will make your job all the more difficult and at times nearly impossible for you to succeed. What could happen is they will say one thing and do another often being rebellious and potentially causing problems for yourself and the success of your work. The goal is to have a certain degree of respect to maintain and grow relationships.

You are working on behalf of your stakeholders and your organization. You need to protect the interests of the organization and your project, programs, or portfolio from any wrongdoing, which may stem from your own actions. There is an implicit trust placed on you in your job and the tasks that need to happen to realize your goals. Misguiding others (suppliers, colleagues, managers) either directly or indirectly can permanently damage the relationship not just for you but also for others you work with and those that have not even joined the organization yet. It can take great effort over a period of time to obtain the same degree of trust and autonomy so do the due diligence and carry out the work that is in your program or project charter ethically and with the stakeholders and organization in mind. There are situations in which trust cannot be reestablished and the relationship fails, or new people are bought into the pictures to restart the program or project. Although your team does not directly report to you in the organization you are still responsible for their actions while they are working for you on your team. Do not let unacceptable behavior slide to the team member's manager responsibility. There are going to be times where you have to work in partnership in situations where a team member is behaving unethically or in a manner that cause issues for your project, program, or portfolio's work. There may even be situations where the team member's manager is the one behaving unethically, and you need to take this up the chain of command. You may feel uneasy or unsure if you should just let the actions slide. This can be a tricky point for individuals. Your actions can have a lasting effect, and you will have to live with the results. Make an internal decision if the situation aroused that you can do what is necessary, as this is what your organization expects you to do. Talk with your support group and come up with some hypothetical situations that can happen in your role paying attention to how you would react and what actions you would take to remedy the situations.

6.4 Meeting Potential Allies

The concept that everyone you meet is a potential ally may not come naturally to you. Perhaps you had situations in the past where you now make assumptions before you know the real facts. You assumed that someone or a group might not cooperate with you before you could verify their intentions. Relearning that people are inherently good and want to cooperate even when there may be some suggestions to show otherwise will benefit you and your team. There can be so much that you have to work overtime in a project, program, or within your portfolio why make it harder by having false beliefs? Take the burden off yourself and place all your energy on your future and current allies. There is no foreseeable benefit of worrying or playing out situations in your head when the interactions did not take place. When you are introduced to someone either in person or virtually, you make a judgment within 30 seconds of that person's potential interest with you, the degree to which you can trust him or her, and if you "like" him or her. Before this book discusses assessing someone else, you need to look at yourself. The phrase "seek to understand then be understood" is one that you need to grasp the concept in order to begin to form allies.

People remember how you make them feel longer than what you said to them. Think back to an earlier stage in your career. Can you think of how someone made you feel special or someone who upset you? The memory is current, and if you tried to remember the specific details of what was said you would have to put some more effort in bringing back those memories. How can you take this and translate it into actionable actions when you meet someone for the first time? First, come prepared. Not knowing key details or people's names and job titles is only going to hurt you in the initial minute or two of the conversation. Show the person or group that you understand their situation and can offer immediate help. Repeat their questions before you provide an answer so they know you were listening and actually do understand what is needed. They will be appreciative of your actions. The location and medium that you choose or agree to meet has a significant impact on how successful you will be in your discussion. If you are going to use a conference room that has a problematic conference phone, for example, they are likely to get frustrated and want to end the discussion sooner, and you will have agreed upon fewer points than you sought out in the first place. Always be prepared, never let something that you can control have the possibility for a negative impact on your relationships. There will be more than enough chances for potential discussion breakdowns and mitigating them before they take place will allow you to have them as allies.

Having regular "check-ins" to assess how the relationship is going not only serves as a purpose to solve any problems but to celebrate successes. Do no wait too long to celebrate with those you deem to be your allies. Keep the momentum, building provides the perfect base for taking your relationships to another level. Sometimes people let the daily work overtake the time to celebrate. A common misconception is saying we have too much on our plate right now and when it dies down we will celebrate. There is always room to dedicate a few hours when there is so much potential positivity that comes out of these events.

Now that the initial meeting took place, how can you turn it into a relationship? First, you need to assess how the discussions went. Tell someone what the other person(s) said, and what you said in return. If you have meeting minutes have your support team look at them so they can help you to a greater degree. Your assessment could be more negatively geared or overlooking missed opportunities. Optionally work with your support team to have mock meetings to see how you do when others are rating you and your style. Your support team is an integral part in your development as a project, program, or portfolio manager in a matrix structure. I hope you see the value this system has for you and that they are not just supporting you, but they are guiding you and letting you test the waters before you make the inter-actions and relationships so you are most prepared and have the great-est chance of success.

6.5 Know Your Audience's World

Your audience's world is one that you have to understand no matter what to be successful in your role. Immerse yourself in it, learn it, and stay current. Using the correct language or industry speak will keep people listening in and giving you all the greater chance to get buy-in to your views Spend the necessary time prior to making a presentation or speech and truly understand the audience members. Aside from knowing your audience's demographic and interests you are making more effective presentations to acquire influence and future success.

When you attend a presentation and really get the topic and the message being discussed you acquire more knowledge and generate more ideas as a result. This is no easy task depending on the topic, venue, medium, and audience knowledge and interest of the topic. There are, however, key takeaways that you can use to make a greater connection to your audience. The greater connections, the more likely they will actively listen to what you have to say and make that connec-tion between presenter and audience member you are seeking. There are the basics such as you speak clearly or follow a set agenda. This book is going to discuss the more captivating and desirable skills and traits that presenters have that you can utilize.

Steve Jobs's presentations on Apple products were truly remarkable moments. The local audience where he presented and the larger global audience were glued to computer screens and smartphones for each word he said in his 60–90 minute presentation. There were things about the way he presented that captured everyone on the smallest details of Apple products. With his trademark black long sleeve shirt and blue jeans he changed the world. You too can change the world for those that you want to influence.

Presenting is about storytelling. First, you give some background on the topic to make your audience more aware of the topic; then you build your momentum having your audience always wanting more.

Presenting done well is not reading off a list or PowerPoint slide nor is it trying to be something you are not. Spend some time to research your favorite presenter or presentation and write down five things they did well and two things you did not like. You are going to use the Post-it notes for the following exercise. Think of a topic that you know quite well. What you are going to do is look at one of the Post-it notes at a time for two minutes, and place emphasis on what is on the Post-it note when you speak. If you liked that the presenter used pauses to control the presentation then you too will create dramatic and meaningful pauses. Once you are done with all five Post-it notes think how you normally present and which version if practiced is better. The gap is what you want to work on improving. Connecting to the audience can be difficult. There can be many hurdles for you to jump over and through to make your audience understand and live your message. Depending on the medium you are using pay particular attention to any obstacles that can come up and correct them before it is too late. Finally, a simple acronym to keep in mind, KNOW (Knowledge, Not, Obstacles, Win), helps to remind you that your knowledge can overcome any obstacle if you are persistent and creative enough. Never let the obstacle stand in the way of you and understanding your audience—there is too much at stake.

6.6 Organizational Currencies

What is the unit of trade in your organization that enables you to influence others? Is it positional power, subject matter expertise, legitimate power, or a combination? The list can go on and the right currency used in the proper situation makes all the difference. This book is going to discuss two themes on the organizational currency topic. First, what currency can a leader control and what is common trade in organizations. A case study has been developed to demonstrate what has been discussed on the topic. This section is paramount to really grasp how you can acquire and use influence in the matrix structure in your organization.

Look at Figure 6.4 (Cohen and Bradford, 2005, p. 95, Table 5.3) and check off where you feel you stand with your present state of being self-aware in your role. Some of the questions you will understand, and some are may be new to you. It is a different way of thinking and

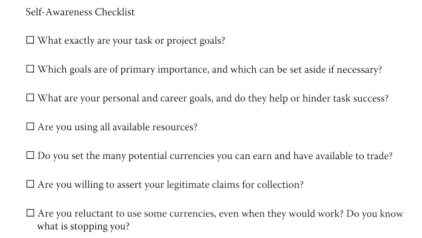

Self-Awareness Checklist

☐ What exactly are your task or project goals?

☐ Which goals are of primary importance, and which can be set aside if necessary?

☐ What are your personal and career goals, and do they help or hinder task success?

☐ Are you using all available resources?

☐ Do you set the many potential currencies you can earn and have available to trade?

☐ Are you willing to assert your legitimate claims for collection?

☐ Are you reluctant to use some currencies, even when they would work? Do you know what is stopping you?

Figure 6.4   Self-awareness checklist. (From Cohen, A. R., and Bradford, D. L., *Influence without Authority*, Wiley & Sons, Hoboken, NJ, 2005, p. 95, Table 5.3. Copyright Wiley-VCH Verlag GmbH & Co. KGaA. Reproduced with permission.)

assessing yourself and others. See if you are able to have some members in your organization fill it out also for completeness and to give you a more 360° view of your self-awareness level. Did you know that being self-aware enables you to influence those who are important to you in your projects, programs, or portfolio? Being self-aware is not a tick in the box type of activity; there is work that needs to be done on your part on an ongoing basis. Have you ever had conversations at work where the themes were similar to the checklist? Try writing five of your own questions that are specific to your current or future situation. Work with one of the members of your support team and really take a look at self-awareness needs and current level of understanding.

6.6.1 *Currencies Frequently Valued in Organizations*

This chapter examines and discusses four frequently valued currencies in the organization. These four are among the most important and widely used currencies for most situations that you will be in. What you the reader have to do is be able to translate these four currencies into action. Gaining influence and demonstrating authority can be a skill that can be learned. Formal position within the organization itself gains a minimal level of influence. For those who can demonstrate task-related, position-related, relationship-related, and personal currencies that no matter where in the organizational chart they sit, there is always the ability to influence at all levels inside the organization and outside. As a project, program, or portfolio manager you have certain currencies that you can immediately apply within your role and organization. Perhaps you need team members to influence others for your tasks in addition to your needs.

Table 6.1 presents a more comprehensive list of organizational currencies. Several of these currencies will now be discussed in detail. These currencies are task-related, position-related, relationship-related, and personal currencies. What is important to understand is you are able to position yourself and utilize the various currencies depending on your objectives and audience. Look back at past situations that have been challenging and ones that you face regularly. How can you incorporate these currencies into your professional life? It may be helpful to make a list so you can better remember which ones you want to rely on more than others.

6.6.1.1 Task-Related Currencies   As a project, program, or portfolio manager you are in a unique position that can trade you and your team's assistance, resources, and expertise to another individual or group with the goal to gain that person's influence. This currency is powerful, and when managed wisely can enable you to gain influence over your followers. When you are thinking about how to establish this currency in your arsenal keep the following realities in mind. Resources, whether they are people or a physical or virtual object, are always scarce and over allocating can hurt you in the future when you need to count on that resource again. Never ask for too much and never give too little. If you follow this saying you will not erode your resource base and justifyingly so not under deliver to those whom you wish to influence. Task-related currencies are about cooperation and working together with external members of your team. They are about information and the sharing and transparency that you allow. To use this currency you have to have others interests aligned with yours and vice versa. As discussed, the onset of a relationship to a certain degree dictates how the relationship will perform. If both parties are dishonest in initial meetings then how can you expect to have a degree of

Table 6.1 Currencies Frequently Valued in Organizations

INSPIRATION-RELATED CURRENCIES	
Vision	Being involved in a task that has larger significances for unit, organization, customers, or society
Excellence	Having a change to do important things really well
Moral/ethical correctness	Doing what is "right" by a higher standard than efficiency
TASK-RELATED CURRENCIES	
New resources	Obtaining money, budget increases, personnel, space, and so forth
Challenge/learning	Getting to do tasks that increase skills and abilities
Assistance	Receiving help with existing projects or unwanted tasks
Organizational support	Receiving overt or sublet backing or direct assistance with implementation
Rapid response	Getting something more quickly
Information	Obtaining access to organizational or technical knowledge
POSITION-RELATED CURRENCIES	
Recognition	Acknowledgment of effort, accomplishment, or abilities
Visibility	The chance to be known by higher-ups or significant others in the organization
Reputation	Being seen as competent, committed
Insiderness/importance	A sense of centrality, of belonging
Contracts	Opportunities for linking with others
Relationship-related currencies	
Understanding	Having concerns and issues listened to
Acceptance/inclusion	Feeling closeness and friendship
Personal support	Receiving personal and emotional backing
PERSONAL-RELATED CURRENCIES	
Gratitude	Appreciation or expression of indebtedness
Ownership/involvement	Ownership of and influence over important tasks
Self-concept	Affirmation of values, self-esteem, and identity
Comfort	Avoidance of hassles

Source: Cohen, A. R., and Bradford, D. L., *Influence without Authority*, Wiley & Sons, Hoboken, NJ, 2005, p. 95, Table 5.3. Copyright Wiley-VCH Verlag GmbH & Co. KGaA. Reproduced with permission.

trust with this person? A relationship based on deception may never take off and blossom.

How else can you in your job utilize task-based currencies? If you challenge your team in their tasks they will not only be more engaged, but you can gain their cooperation. A lot has been discussed about gaining stakeholder, functional manager, and other outside cooperation and now cooperation from within your team. You have more interactions with your team than you do with any other group for your projects, programs, and portfolio. Your team should be the mold that you want to transfer onto other groups and individuals. The core team that you work with is responsible for creating the bulk of your work. A good gauge is 80% of your output comes from your core team members. The need to not only influence this group but capture all challenges and rectify them as soon as possible will not allow for issues to bleed to your outer team and stakeholders. You can now see how this is a balancing act that is not a one-time occurrence. It requires regular maintenance to sustain and grow.

When you influence someone or a group you can get them to work on your agenda. This lessens the burden that you have and allows for a healthy mix of give and take. An important thought is what if I spend all my time trying to please others with the hope of gaining influence, and it affects my work? Think strategically and look at the top three groups or individuals that affect the majority of your projects, programs, or portfolio. If you allocate yourself to areas that have little to marginal return you are going to lose out on big players and influencers. It is often a novice mistake to want to please everyone equally. If you look to gain a lot, spend a lot. If there is chance for future influence, work on that group or individuals but do not over utilize you or your team's effort. The definition of strategy is a plan of action to achieve overall aim. It does not assume 100% obtainment of your goal. This goal should always be pursued but when you look at your calendar and your teams you realize that you only have so much time and so many resources that can be allocated to any given activity. The good part is you are in a job function that deals with these types of challenges regularly so the chance that you are proficient is quite high.

6.6.1.2 Position-Related Currencies   One way to gain the influence of your team members or outsiders is to understand that people value recognition and visibility within the organization. They want others to see the work they have done and hear the feedback accordingly. Does the nature of your team's work allow for others to see the progression and final results? If the nature of your work is sensitive in nature and does not allow you or your team to share the results or progress, share it within your team, and let outsiders know their level of contribution and how it impacted the organization. Again just as a task-related currency was not a foreign concept, position-related currencies should come easy to you in your role in a matrix structure.

This is your chance to be a cheerleader for your team and projects, programs, and portfolio. You are to make public to stakeholders, functional managers, and others the contributions your core and extended team members made. Never withhold congratulation when one is earned. Make it memorable when you make congratulations. Do not overuse this currency or it will become devalued. You need to be aware of the actual work being done and any obstacles that were overcome. When you have team meetings take the time to have the individual describe the work he or she did and how it was done. These meetings are also a good chance for your team to learn new methods to troubleshoot and acquire additional knowledge. When possible, offer rewards such as lunch with the CEO or key stakeholders on your projects, programs, or portfolio. Do something that is not just a "thank you." You do not have to be elaborate but be creative and depending on the person do what makes sense for that particular situation and accomplishment that was made. It is completely possible to use position-related currencies to thank someone for something they did in the past; you do not have to wait for something to happen. If you are going to thank several people do not do a carbon copy of each thank you for each person. Customized and personalize thank you notes. They come from you and reflect on the organization when you give one. Remember people remember how you make them feel longer than what you said or what physical gift was given.

6.6.1.3 Relationship-Related Currencies   One of the basic needs of humans is to belong and feel welcome in the groups to which they belong. For your situation this also includes being connected to the organization not just with team members. Often people can feel disconnected in the organization, they may not even know the name of the person who sits across from them let alone what they do on a day-to-day basis. Look to your human resource department to see what is available or recommended for your situation if this is the case. An important point has to be made. You can only go so far alone, and one of the pillars of this book is utilizing others to accomplish your goals in a mutual beneficial relationship. The age of one person doing everything on his or her own without others help has long gone. The modern organization is too complex, and the velocity is too fast to make do alone. When you try to do everything on your own you marginalize your success, effectiveness, and reach within the organization.

Making use of technology, such as Microsoft SharePoint for collaboration or Microsoft Yammer for informal team communications, is one way the modern influencer is embracing and exploiting this challenge. There should be no viable reason that your team does not feel connected and engaged in their roles. If there are gaps in the organization you should be able to cover them with low to moderate level of effort. Using active listening to hear the problems your team members are facing allow for appropriate corrective action and thought as to how to prevent this type of problem in the future. Never miss an opportunity to answer someone's question. Perhaps have a town hall once a month that discusses everything from where the organization is going at high level all the way down to individual tasks from your team. Consistency is key and missing an opportunity to thank someone or have a town hall can quickly erode all efforts that you have made to date and in the future. Come up with a strategy that is viable and effective on how you will recognize and thank your team members as well as outsiders and stakeholders. Your efforts will allow for team members to be more appreciative for the work opportunity they have been given and for any help along the way from their coworkers.

6.6.1.4 Personal-Related Currencies   Personal currencies are perhaps the simplest of the five currencies that you will encounter. It should be noted that this does not mean you should negate others who require more effort or time.

Personal currencies can be simply showing gratitude to someone. Giving them the freedom to make their own decisions and see through their commitments. If you were to not allow for autonomy within your team, you will soon find that you are spending almost all your time on tasks that can be delegated to someone else, and you will lose sight of the big picture then the real problems will begin. Team members will become disengaged and robotic in their view and actions when working on your projects, programs, or portfolio. Is this process fair for my team members? Will this allow for feedback from

other team members and others on this project? These are key question to ask yourself when you do an activity that affects someone in
your team, functional managers, stakeholders, and people outside of
your organization.

6.7 The Modern Influencer

A modern influencer is someone in the organization who is at the
hub of knowledge, influence, and understanding of the organization's
goals and vision. He or she drives change and harmony among divi-
sional groups and team members. To be a modern influencer you have
to make certain contributions to shape the organization. This can be
accomplished through introducing new knowledge, launching a new
product or service, or leading through difficult times. There is a short-
age of influencers who tackle these challenges, and as a project, program, or portfolio manager you will have this opportunity. Your role
often deals with work of this type and is often visible to multiple organizational groups and executives. One of the outputs of being a modern influencer is you see the work to its finish. Often when a leader
in a matrix structure takes on an opportunity, he or she owns that
issue until completion. Seeing the work reach its final destination is
rewarding in itself not to mention hearing the feedback of the effected
users of your project, program, or portfolio. The modern influencer
does some investigating into areas but does a lot of listening to those
affected. It is this activity of engaging others' participation and not
solely focusing on self-analysis that keeps the momentum for change
happening. Momentum although may be hard to start often is just as
hard to slow down and stop once some speed and velocity increases.
To be a modern influencer you have to seek the buy-in of subject-
matter experts, trusted employees, and senior executives. It is only
then that you will have the playing field to tackle the opportunities
that need to be addressed in your projects, programs, and portfolio.

The modern influencer does not solely rely on himself or herself to
lead the change, he or she takes juniors in the organization and mentor them to lead smaller but important aspects of the vision. Although
the modern influencer is capable of doing all the work on his or her
own, the value of synergies by bringing others on board increases
the stickiness of the efforts and goals. Junior members are more than

willing and often seeking leadership challenges that make an ideal partnership with you. Never give them too much that can damage your work but not too little that a little stretch can be felt with their capabilities. Making your vision and goals stick in an organization can often be more challenging and questionable as to how to achieve it than the initial drive for change. The SWOT analysis credit comes from two Harvard Business School Policy Unit professors—George Albert Smith Jr. and C. Roland Christiensen during the early 1950s, which may surprise some people with Michael Porter being so associated with the tool. It should be known that another HBS Policy Unit professor Kenneth Andrews developed its usage and application. All professors were specialists in organizational strategy as opposed to marketing. SWOT went on to be developed by the HBS during the 1960s until SWOT became the tool we use today. Before engaging we will allow you to see a more complete and in-depth picture of the environment you will be attacking. This analysis is an example of mandatory planning that you, a project, program, or portfolio manager understand and can thrive to develop. Being able to see the trees from the forest enables you to dive in on any sticking points in your execution. You understand the need for planning and thrive in visualizing the future. In a matrix structure with such variety among people who you will interact with it goes without questioning on the importance of planning communications and executions. Small errors can stay a long time and discourage those in your team and yourself.

6.8 Four Things Really Persuasive People Do

Really persuasive people rally the troops, set the team direction, and engage everyone involved seeking to use the collective group to solve problems and make improvements. It does not go without question that understanding that utilizing your team and those in your projects, programs, or portfolio is a competitive advantage not just for your work that you have to do but for overcoming your obstacles that you face. It is inevitable that there will be obstacles along the way. If there were no challenges faced from start to finish there would not be the need for leadership. This is far from reality. Having purpose and wanting to put in the effort enables you to reach the finish line before those who do not have the drive to keep going when there are challenges or there are no visible signs of progress. The inner hunger and drive comes from a sense of belonging and commitment to your organization and team. Someone with purpose knows exactly why he or she is in the role they are in and how this person and the organization can use this purpose to instill it in others. Those with purpose are more willing to commit and take on responsibilities.

Listening can come in two forms: active and passive. Active listening is when you look for underlying connections and patterns in your communications. You are looking for not just what is being said but what is not being said taking notice of body language and the environment around you. Passive listening is mechanical and effortless. It relies on being self-ware and understanding those around you and the way they work and communicate. It does not require any special effort. Passive listening is what most people do but does not yield as much as a result as active listening, which requires more on your part. Acknowledging others is an activity that does not cost anything but yields a payback that you can continue to reap the rewards long after the compliment is made. Taking a genuine effort and interest in those whom you acknowledge is par for the course. You must show and demonstrate genuine interest; otherwise, the compliment does not mean much and perhaps can cause resentment as it may not appear to be genuine. Knowing how to cooperate and not needing to win every war is something really persuasive people do all the time. There is no need to strive to win every battle when you are concerned with winning the war. It can go against you and perhaps hurt your progress and goals. Being humble no matter how successful you are takes practice and having your support team keep you grounded will make for better relations with others in your projects, programs, or portfolio.

6.9 Influence Styles

When discussing influence it is not just good practice but it is essential to know your style that you use in various situations as well as recognizing others for the topic that is being discussed at the moment or in a future conversations. This is a part of being self-aware and knowing your surroundings. You may not be used to such formality and may feel it is not effective as you would have wanted. Perhaps you feel it is not natural, and you are better off doing what you have, which may not be optimal but it "works" for you. Through practice you will change and improve. Taking calculated baby steps in the direction of mastering the five influence styles you will see greater buy in from others and greater influence ability. There are five main influence styles that you as a leader can use as you try to assert influence over your followers, team members, management, and clients. These five styles are as follows: asserting, convincing, negotiating, bridging, and inspiring respectfully. You may be wondering if you can have parts of more than one style that you show, but it should be understood that you use one dominant style in a given situation. This book is now going to look at some characteristics of each of the five styles to provide insight into your styles that you use.

Asserting, however, states that you always have others listen to your ideas and are almost always challenging others when exchanging ideas and points of views. Challenging others has a genuine use such as probing when trying to understand a situation or topic but overuse can in fact cause harm to your position and level of influence. This can lead to a breakdown in the conversation so challenge others wisely and with purpose in mind. The five influence types are tools that when used enable you to achieve your goal in influencing others. They should be "kept" with you at all times and expanding on your weaknesses overtime will enable you to be a strong influencer no matter the audience or topic on hand. If you are trying a new technique or style that you do not use often pick a low importance conversation with someone who is not going to cause you harm if you make any mistakes. Once you master the style or technique you can use it where the stakes are higher. Always keep in mind good intentions do not translate into cooperation. Learning how best to use a style will enable you to not make these beginner mistakes and when there may not be a chance to practice. I will now continue on and discuss the remaining three influence styles.

When you are using the convincing style it convinces you to use reason and logic to convey to others your thoughts. You make sound judgments and logic in your arguments. You listen actively to others trying to find the real meaning of their comments and questions.

The third style is the negotiating style, which looks to make compromises and is interested in satisfying the greater interest of the group not just your agenda. At first glance some may feel this style is for weak leaders and they must have their voice heard and action taken accordingly. If people are not following your instructions you may wonder how you can be successful. On the contrary, in a matrix structure you will in fact be doing a lot of compromising as you will be dealing with people who have competing interests and goals. There often will be shared resources that are being discussed, and as mentioned your goal is to win the war not the battle. It is in your advantage to make note to others when you compromised and bring it up when you are asking something from them. By showing that you were willing to cooperate when they needed you on their side they will more than likely be there for you. It should be discussed that if you find that a person or group always asks for cooperation but never returns the favor you need to look and examine the organizational currencies that matter to them that will enable you to influence those people and groups. This chapter discussed four types of organizational currency: task, position, relationship, and personal. Understand how to utilize these tools and when you are in such a situation you will have a high chance of success. There is strategy in play when you exchange something to someone or a group that wants and or needs it. If you always are ethical and honest you have a greater chance of the favor being returned when you are on the other side of the bargaining table. You will make a name for yourself as an honest and ethical person who has everyone's intentions on the table and addresses all of them. In the end very few people will not return favors that are within reason and have had good relations with that person.

The bridging influence style focuses on connecting others through active listening and building coalitions. This style is useful while you work in a matrix structure. It comes in handy and is practical when working with people from different organizational groups or teams. Often you will find yourself in the position that bridges the gap among diverse groups of individuals in your organization. You have to understand how to communicate in the language that matters to your audience to get their full attention and support. Not doing this is a large mistake, which will limit your success when using the bridging influence style. Finally, there is the inspiring influence style that asserts your own position while encouraging others and aims to build a shared purpose to influence others. You will often have to influence others, which is the topic of a large number of your discussions with your team and other organizational groups at your company. Shared purpose and vision should be straightforward. If it seems complex take out some of the layers and think of three bulleted points that describe the shared purpose of the individuals you are trying to influence. Writing it down helps you see the big picture and avoids lengthy sentences and jargon that may come up.

Each style is suited for specific situations. It is not advisable to always have the same position but rather adjust to your audience and surroundings depending on what you are trying to achieve. In fact, you are doing yourself and others harm by always taking the same style. Sometimes we get comfortable with a style and rely on it more than we should. Take small steps at not critical times to explore one of the other styles till you become comfortable using it in everyday business. It should be noted that discussion on influence styles should be a starting point that you investigate, which one you normally use and how successful it has been working out for you in the past. When you see improvement in your influence ability you will achieve greater results and drive change among individuals that perhaps resist change.

6.10 Conclusion

This chapter focused on an important and useful area of personal self-improvement and discovery for you in your role in a matrix structure. At the start of the chapter defining and prioritizing were discussed to serve as a starting point that you examined and to assist you in gaining influence over your followers. You cannot gain influence over others if you do not have them on board with your agenda. You learned that sometimes your agenda means incorporating parts or points of views of others with the greater goal of cooperation and long-term commitment. You also learned how to prepare for an exchange as you learned your audience's world and what is important to them. You can be the more strategic negotiator but not knowing what the other person feels is important can risk not getting their cooperation and influence. A concept of the modern influencer was discussed as a way to assist you to achieve. Even if you are a while away from the definition of a modern influencer is something that you should strive to achieve.

CURRENCIES YOU CONTROL THAT ARE VALUABLE TO ANY BOSS

Performing above and beyond what is required is a traditional way of building credits with any boss, but it is still fundamental. When Les Charm asked to work directly at finding unusual, profitable loan opportunities and then delivered, he was given extraordinary latitude by a manager who appreciated the results and was willing to bend the results to accommodate a star performer who provided more than expected. Not having to worry about the subordinate's area, knowing he or she will deliver, as Les Charm did when he found new customers.

(From Cohen, A., and Bradford, D., 2005, p. 91, Table 5.2)

You have to build "credits" though performing what is required and beyond should not be overlooked. Over delivering on expectations of your clients and your managers are one of the oldest and most common but least understood ways to acquire someone's influence. It should go without saying this method should be in your toolbox and used in conjunction with what this chapter has discussed.

Case Study

The Chapter 6 case study looks at organizational currency at a practical level to show its strengths, what is required by you, and possible weak points that you will encounter in your organization and team. This case study will examine two people within the same organization. Michael Radford and Mary Jo McCallion have been with MNP Inc., a professional service firm—Michael with 10 years' experience and Mary Jo with roughly 3 years—and they both were hired and reside in the New York, New York office. Mary Jo works in human resources, while Michael works as an information technology (IT) project manager. Mary Jo has been

promoted to a human resource project manager in charge of leading a large human resource information system (HRIS) project.
Her past role as a human resource manager enabled her to have the
visibility of the human resource arm for the office of 225 people.
She earned her respect through a no-nonsense approaches with
a personal touch. Michael works in the information technology
consulting division. He has had some challenges and along the
way with people on his team and others from different groups
within the organization and is facing a tough project implementing a project management information system (PMIS) for a multinational organization, TNJ Worldwide, based in Las Vegas,
Nevada. This case study is going to examine both Mary Jo's and
Michael's situations and how organizational currency could make
their projects more manageable and the relationships of those they
interact with more fruitful and stable in difficult times.

Michael and Mary Jo both work a matrix structure as their
organization uses it as it provides the benefits of shared resources.
Michael has a moderate sized team consisting of nine resources
internally with a mix of professionals and administrative members
that execute his projects across three departments. Mary Jo works
with the human resource department and has a few key stakeholders within the organization who are business leaders and are
often only available for limited time periods. Making the best use
of their time (in person or in writing) is crucial to accomplishing
her tasks. She has challenges since her resources often are unavail-
able to work on her HRIS project as they are often working on
other projects that their manager's feel is more important. This is
the first time her organization is implementing a HRIS system of
this size and complexity. It is key to get buy-in from the organization if this system will be adopted once delivered. Michael's PMIS
project is replacing an old system that had seen better days. Users
are constantly complaining of the lack of functionality and limited
capabilities. He has one year to deliver the new solution. Mary Jo's
project, on the contrary, has to be delivered in six months. Both
have unique and similar challenges in the next one year and six
months respectfully.

Michael's contact at TNJ Worldwide, however, has not giving him the necessary time to scope out the project requirements.

How can Michael get more cooperation and ongoing support? Michael needs to examine the relationship with those whom he works with that are giving him challenges. He writes down where the pain points are and consults with a friend who had similar challenges but managed to excel with his projects. He found that many people in organizations trade currencies like money that have different values. They are able to bridge the gap from his problems to his goals with his team and client contacts. Michael has to gain the trust of the user base and at the same time get the necessary level of cooperation and input from his client contact. He worked at improving his position-related currency reputation appealing his 10 years of experience in project management. He hosted town halls that shed light on the new system. He discussed its timeline and what the final product will look like. He provided his contact information to keep an open door to communications regarding the progression of the project. He went back and incorporated some of the suggestions from the town hall and informed those who made the initial suggestion that their ideas were used. A company-wide accessible web page was established within TNJ Worldwide that showed the progress of the project to keep employees and stakeholders in the loop. He used this web page to gain operational support from the internal IT department and the PMO staff who would be the primary users of the PMIS system. Enabling others to take part in the overall vision of the PMIS enables greater cooperation and support when asked and needed.

For Michael's team there were several members to whom he had to emphasize task-related currencies such as providing a challenge and learning opportunity. By his team working on this new PMIS project enabled them to learn a new skill and work with different clients and internal coworkers. Showing this opportunity is what was needed for cooperation and mutual goal sharing among the team. He has to appeal to a department manager's personal-related currency for gratitude in lending and maxing out his resources that Michael could utilize. Michael was often faced in situations that required overtime by team members and a heavy workload.

Mary Jo had led the human resource department previously as the HR manager. In her new role as a human resource project manager her first project was to implement a HRIS. Mary Jo has had experience with two HRIS vendors in the past, but this project will be much larger and visible then any project she has worked on to date. Mary Jo went through her internal rolodex prior to commencing work in an effort to get buy in and form a relationship with her key resources and those in the IT department she will be interacting with on her project. Mary Jo is utilizing organizational currency without even knowing it. She is using multiple currencies such as task-related (organizational support) and position-related. Mary has excelled in a work field that is often taken second seat to the other departments as the human resource function has changed over the years and decades concerning its importance in the organization. Learning how to maintain relationships and not see ones that are do not sour over time keeps her in touch and others available when she needs their cooperation and vice versa. Mary Jo knows it is a two-way street as no relationship works when it is all take and no give. She solicits volunteers for help for others' tasks and special projects where she can make a contribution. She brings in new talent from the organization and offers new people a spot at the table to make a contribution. Mary Jo's challenge of working with an over-utilized team emphasized common goals, the bigger picture, small goals, and recognition. All of these aspects are a part of organizational currency.

Michael and Mary Jo both ended up delivering their projects, but learned a dollar means different things to different people and is valued differently. What is important for the person you are talking to is what makes a partnership succeed, sustain, and grow? Being practical and proficient with taking the time to personally follow up with tasks is what gets the job done. This case study examined two different and similar people both working on projects. Both happened to be technology focused, but one was from the human resource department and the other from the professional service arm of the organization. Anyone in the organization can benefit from organizational currencies, but it is especially true for a project, program, or portfolio managers in a matrix structure because of the organization type and job function combined. It should be known that organizational currencies are not all that is needed but are a tool that is beneficial from day one using it. It does not need saying this tool should be in your arsenal as soon as possible but no later than the onset of a project, program, or your portfolio.

CASE STUDY DISCUSSION QUESTIONS

- What is the opportunity that Michael and Mary Jo were presented with?
- What played a role in each of Michael's and Mary Jo's successes?
- Are there any noneconomic risks?
- How has influence affected the outcome of each of their projects?
- What kind of follow-up should Michael and Mary Jo make to their success?

SUMMARY CHECKLIST

- Make clear goals that you have for your projects, programs, and portfolio that show where you require influence.
- Recognize organizational currency and how it can directly benefit you in your role and the various types of currencies available.
- Learn to think strategically in your communications and what it takes to be really persuasive.

7

LEADERSHIP PERCEPTIONS FOR THOSE WITHOUT AUTHORITY

Looking back at Chapter 1 and the mind map of influential leaders you created (see Figure 7.1), how do you currently stand with your identified skills for improvement, leadership traits, and your overall progress? As in the other chapters, this mind map starts each chapter by providing a guide on what this book teaches and to give you the opportunity to compare your goals and progress along your journey. Always have an open discussion with your group on where you stand and whether you are having any roadblocks.

This chapter's goal is to provide different views and perceptions that you and others will have of your role as a project, program, or portfolio manager in a matrix structure. It is important not only to learn tools and tactics but also reflect of yourself and others in your communications and interactions within the workplace. The purpose of reflection is recollection and asking you to consider the choices you made and the outcomes they produced. It goes without saying that doing what you always did will yield the same result. How can you expect to grow and improve if you do not take reflection seriously? You cannot make meaningful change by trying harder at the same things in the same ways. Reflection is not always just about what happened in the past but what you want to do in the future. It should not be done sporadically but daily perhaps in the morning or evening. Create a calm and peaceful area that you can perform your reflections without interruption. This chapter will take a look at several capacities for further reflection and learning. It is with this new knowledge and skill that you will be more effective in leading in a matrix structure.

Figure 7.1   Mind map of influential leaders.

7.1 The Impact of Leadership Perception Style and Use of Power

I can ask you to get me a document from the filing cabinet and have an expectation that you will comply. What is it that makes you get the document? Was it that it took little effort, perhaps I got a document for your earlier, or you formally report to me and are obliged to do so. In a matrix structure you may not have the ability to rely on someone's obligations to comply with your request. As Chapter 3 outlined the six bases of power now you get to reflect and understand the uses of power that are available to you in your situation. Using the least impactful and most effective method is one that will cause a continuous tug of war. Overusing power or overusing a certain power base can affect future participation by the individual(s). Practice and experience will allow for greater success and knowing what power base to utilize and when will assist in this quest. If you are on the receiving end of power you are more likely to accept it if someone appeals to your interests, common goals, and provides a "what's in it for me" aspect. If you were able to build a rapport previously or at the moment you asked for something, cooperation is greatly increased.

7.2 Analysis of 360° Feedback

When you go through a 360° feedback in your workplace you are assessing your leadership capabilities foremost for a project, program, or portfolio manager. The groups that participate in this feedback are your manager, team members, yourself, peers, and those who have worked on any of your projects, programs, and portfolio. The major output of a 360° feedback is an action plan. Your support team already is there for you to provide you with what is needed for your improvement in your job function while working in a matrix structure. A 360° feedback that is not effective in creating an action plan that makes the person accountable to their improvement lacks the rigor and buy-in within the organization. There has to be support across the organization that this process is more than a few interviews and filling out some documents. Real change has to occur and that often comes with some conflict of opinions and views. Understanding that there will be on occasion some challenges to questions or answers provides a safe environment for everyone involved to ask the real question and make decisions. All parties should come prepared, and though the course of the period the 360° is measuring there should be continuous feedback and expected improvement. The 360° feedback mechanism should not surprise or "unload" on any person. It should go without saying that there should be no major new news from either party during the feedback sessions. Dealing with what happens "in the field" provides immediate feedback on a positive action or suggestion on how to correct oneself for a future action of this type. The 360° feedback should provide highlights of the instantaneous feedback that occurred and summarize it for both parties so there is further agreement on how to proceed for the future. It should be noted that most effective 360° feedback processes are ones that are anonymous totally, so the followers do not rate the person so favorably.

The 360° feedbacks although not new are not that old in management training. Generations ago there was no need for more than the direct manager or supervisor to provide feedback. We must remember especially in the role of a project, program, or portfolio manager you have a customer, internal or external you have a customer. You deliver results, you are accountable. Within a matrix there can be highly complex reporting structures and the manager to employee feedback is not sufficient. The business leaders have told the customer they are delivering results that matter, and 360° feedbacks are one tested way that work in such structures across industries and team sizes.

7.3 Perception vs. Reality

How does the leader actually know one's perception of him or herself? Rarely can one be the judge of one's own work accurately. Followers are often going to rate you in a positive light; likewise there may be those that always take a negative spin on your accomplishments as a project, program, or portfolio manager. Looking for a follower or member of your team that provides honest feedback not withstanding any 360° feedback sessions you can learn your true performance judged by your closest peers. Taking out all compliments can lead to discovering your real performance. When your critics are complimenting you then you know your work is top notch. Not ignoring critics is often hard and unpleasant, but those individuals often provide the information you really do need to improve. There is truth in almost anything someone says. Looking for hidden meanings can be confusing and not the best way to spend your time, but reflection on what someone says is the only way you will grasp what needs to be corrected. There is always place for a second opinion, but you need to become effective enough to know when you indeed need a second opinion or can rely on yourself. There is some discomfort in this process with any gaps that exist. There are leaders who have been a leader for decades and who still do not know the difference between perception and reality. The sooner you master this skill you will become a more competent and complete project, program, or portfolio manager. The goal of this book is, slow and steady with little rework wins the race. Speedy progress is often riddled with errors and mine holes waiting for you to find them along your journey.

7.4 Establishing Followership for Leaders without Authority

Establishing a wide and disperse followership for the project, program, or portfolio manager in some instances can take years. Culture, demographics, hierarchy, past experiences, and management styles all play a key role in how much and how successful a leader is in obtaining followers. Looking at existing successful relationships where quick wins can be made is often the starting point. Look for those who are lacking a leader and fill the need. You as the project, program, and portfolio manager should take the phase "crawl before you walk" into account. Making mistakes early on can limit the future success of the group or coalition. Grow followers at a steady pace so you can take your time and not rush, which is noticeable to others. This shows you do not value the individual and just want to collect followers. Even a small group or coalition can produce outstanding results. Take a look at startup technology companies. Several people around a kitchen table can end up having millions of users. The notion that the number of followers is more important than the results is not one that you want to follow. Learn to be satisfied with slow and steady progress. You want to shy away from large variations in new and existing followers. This is always an area that can cause great challenges, and mistakes can be magnified.

7.5 Cross-Cultural Variations in Leadership Perception

Without discussing every cultural difference that can exist in leadership perception this book will reflect and examine on a few key areas. Formality, hierarchy, respect, and "the way things get done here" are among several variations that you can run into when discussing leadership perception. Not learning before acting is almost certain failure in these instances. Failure can have a greater or lesser impact than you may have though in the first place. It is best to seek out someone or read in the culture prior to making decisions that affect such people and groups. Failure can limit your future success and your successor's future success. Always think twice and act once when you interact with different cultures. It is important to note that cultures in this book's case mean organizational and ethnic cultures. Both apply to the project, program, and portfolio manager role.

7.6 Leadership and Self-Perception

The historical view of leader's self-perception is often seen in a positive light. The many rewards are listed and displayed for everyone to see. In reality, there is no further false belief that leaders always view themselves in a positive light. There are often periods of loneliness and discomfort that can be hard to manage at times. There may be no viable option to go to for counsel and often involve making difficult decisions where the outcomes are not always clear. Bearing responsibility wears people out and are in need of rejuvenation on an ongoing basis to keep followers aligned. Leaders for the most part look up to other leaders (business, religious, family, etc.) for direction and guidance. They have an internal belief that their work has purpose, meaning and helps the greater good. This almost irrational drive at times is what is called for when leading in challenging times.

Without this inner drive and belief, their followership will eventually fade and collapse. Not everyone can be a true leader. Bill George, the former CEO of Medtronic and Harvard University Professor, held the belief at a young age that he would be a CEO. His father encouraged him that he could run a large organization such as Coca-Cola or IBM at a young age. His journey was not a direct path to the CEO's office and had setbacks, but his internal drive and mentoring at a young age played a role in his career path and trajectory. He envisioned and worked at achieving this single goal throughout the course of his career. Bill George used mindfulness to guide his leadership style throughout his career. Mindfulness's true meaning and application can be seen as the practice of paying attention to what is going around you and within you in the present time for the individual. For Bill George mindfulness has kept his internal compass focusing on the important tasks at hand and letting what is not in his control not interfere with his decision making.

7.7 Charisma Authority

For those leaders who display charisma there is less of an initial challenge to acquire and retain followers. It should be noted that there is no magic bullet and trying to obtain charisma more than likely will backfire in the leaders' overall effort to acquire and retain their followers. Having role models is important for any leader, but being original in your style will do more than trying to be something that you are not or to display qualities that you did not master. Charisma authority refers to certain quality of a leaders' personality that sets them apart from other leaders that is viewed as supernatural or exceptional powers or qualities. A charismatic leader has an uncanny ability to articulate a complex vision of where the group is headed and why while gaining the majority of the group's agreement. There is a concept in existence called charismatic succession where all the power and authority surrounds the leader needs to be transferred in situations where succession of the leader is necessary. The project, program, or portfolio manager can utilize this style when there are larger groups, or if they are very dispersed over geographic locations. Passing on charisma to key members of your coalition or group enables greater flexibility and smoother operations when there is much change and complexity. If you, as the project, program, or portfolio manager, do not display charismatic approach focus on your strengths. Focus on what you can contribute to the group or coalition. Contrary to popular belief, leaders are successful who lack the charismatic appeal.

Putting unnecessary pressure to imitate a leader you know who displays charisma comes off as fake and can be easily seen though by your followers. Appreciating yourself for your skills is a good role model to others who look up to you. Leaders who are real are more relatable and viewed as trustworthy. Although this section is called "Charisma Authority," much emphasis is placed on NOT being charismatic if you do not have the qualities. Just as dressing in clothes that do not reflect your true self or wearing expensive jewelry to impress others, this approach is a recipe for disaster that can be transferred from you to your followers who imitate your leadership style.

7.8 The Follower's View of a Leader without Authority

For a follower to follow a leader there *always* has to be a reason to do so. Perhaps it is how to work through difficult situations or ones that have not been encountered before. Charisma may attract followers but *results* keep them a follower for the long term. Followers look up to the leader for key signals on how to act and make decisions. When the leader does not have formal authority in the organization, these signals require another piece, which is proof, validation, and influence. There must be some proof that if the follower does what the leader suggests the outcome will be as expected. The validation comes from prior work that demonstrated the leader's experience on the topic at hand, while utilizing influence leaders sway the follower point of view to their needs and goals. Along this process the follower may have doubts and look to poke holes in the leader's plan to see how well it stands up to scrutiny and the follower's values and beliefs. Attracting followers who have been with the organization for many years is in most instances more difficult than those with under a year of work in the organization. There are valid reasons for these views and understanding how to win over the key long-term employees will win the buy-in of the new employees.

There are several groups of followers that you should attempt to attract in a given order. As mentioned, key employees who have been at the company for more than 5 years is your starting point. They require the greatest effort for the most part, and there is no time to waste to start on this group. You will find there are ones that have been waiting for you to come and make change while others resist. As mentioned earlier in this book, the generation-Y employees are among the easiest group to win over and attain support. They lack the negative experiences that members who are more senior have experienced and will spread your mission fast within the lower levels of the organization.

The follower's views may differ from those of the leader they may follow at the same time. They look for different qualities and value. Aligning yourself with whom you want to attract, as followers is just a necessary step to leading others when you do not have formal authority over in the organization. If your values are not aligned commitment will be lacking, and a greater effort on your part will have to be made as a result. A point to mention is the size of the group that the leader has under him or her is always an issue. There is tension among various and diverse points of views, which can affect the direction and agility of the group. When the leader decides to change course much effort and thought has to be made in such instances. Much coordination and time has to be made ensuring everyone can contribute and will consider the views of others. Consideration for separating your followers into separate groups can be an efficient and speedy way to deliver change in organizations. There is no reason for grouping everyone as a whole if there are better options available. When you recognize this concern, the follower may feel without a "home" or disillusioned while groups are formed or changed depending on the leader's vision and mission. Leaders have to be cognizant to have processes in place to ensure no follower falls through the cracks as he or she will become cynical of "the leadership style of today" that is always appearing to change and cause disruption for the individual.

7.9 Conclusion

Leadership cannot be accomplished without followers. This is a rule that cannot be broken. How leaders are viewed by the followers however is up to them to shine light on areas of accomplishment and lessen those on past failures. Followers instantly want to have a leader make the processes easier and show guidance when the options are not so clear or have risk. It is in these situations that the follower latches on with the leader's mantra, and they work together to achieve the mission set forth. The notion of the leader that can do it all on one's own if need be is a falsehood as tasks can reach greater heights and span father distances, therefore, requiring a sense of community and trust to be established and maintained. This piece of the pie can be forgotten but not without penalty as the leader and follower need each other to accomplish the work and satisfy their needs.

Given the opportunity to improve oneself in 360° feedbacks shows a more cohesive picture of the relationship the individual has with the company, project, task, and team. This picture lets the person pinpoint areas to celebrate and those that need improvement. Finding the proper leader and follower up to the challenge remains and will remain an ongoing effort by the organization. These are essential pieces of the puzzle that no internal process or technology can mask. People remain a challenge and opportunity that are worthy to be taken on by the organization.

This chapter discussed many topics that could be a chapter onto themselves depending on your current situation and needs. They provide thought-provoking discussions and areas to look and investigate in your current practices. Ask yourself, what is 80% of the follower's perception of leaders at my company that are in my situation? What matters to them? What works for them and the leader? Leverage existing knowledge and build upon it to form your body of knowledge on followership. When possible seek our past followers and have candid conversations with them in all areas that they can be of help so you can learn from their experiences. Chances are you are going to open doors that have been closed before when people moved on to other opportunities. This approach also is a great chance to rekindle relationships that were once successful or to attempt to improve those that could have shined brighter. The next chapter is the conclusion of this book, which will provide summary and thought-provoking questions for you as the project, program, or portfolio manager.

SUMMARY CHECKLIST

- As a leader, establish a wide and diverse followership.
- Review and understand your perception of your leadership style by your followers.
- Engrain the mantra "leadership cannot be accomplished without followers."
- Engage your manager on having 360° feedback of yourself.

8
CONCLUSION

The purpose of this chapter is to provide insight into what has been discussed in this book and to answer questions on how to proceed as a project, program, or portfolio manager. This book has taken you from the very starting point in your role in a matrix structure along the duration of the role and providing you with thought-provoking awareness about your perception from your followers. There have been case studies throughout the book to discuss a topic in greater detail, test your knowledge, and provide an example or how to apply the knowledge. This book did not cover every topic in the greatest detail level it could, but provides throughout a base and solid understanding of working in a matrix structure. There are many differences than in the classical hierarchical structure and indeed there is much to learn. Without this book you could make common mistakes and run into pitfalls and shortcomings that should certainly be avoided. The summary checklist at the end of each chapter provided the most critical aspects of the chapter to your attention.

Just as there is a difference between management and leadership there is a difference between working as a project, program, or portfolio manager in a standard hierarchical structure. One such difference is the amount of influence you need to have over your team and followers. As they may not formally report to you, getting their cooperation is key to a successful venture. A chapter of this book has been dedicated to the topic of gaining influence. It started from defining your goals and priorities concluding with the various influence styles. Organizational currency is a topic that may be needed and often is foreign to some as one that answers many questions on the what and how of leading without having authority over followers and team members. For further reading on this topic it is highly recommended to obtain a copy of Allan R. Cohen and David L. Bradford's *Influence without Authority*, second edition. Tables from this book were used to discuss organizational currency, and it is worth looking into a greater level of detail. Perhaps, no better examples of how to gain influence for project, program, or portfolio managers can be seen as in this book.

This book started out as a survey of 55 project, program, and portfolio managers asking 13 strategic questions. These questions as outlined in the introduction are themes for this book and have been discussed throughout the book. The survey results of the 55 leaders are in the appendix for those who wish to read each individual answer at that level of detail. The results of the survey provided enough questions that need to be answered in any additional areas that have not been discussed. The book's appendix contains the complete survey.

It is beneficial to examine what was stated in the introduction for reflection and understanding if this learning has occurred for you. Several examples were provided that hopefully you can apply to your organizational life. This was not meant to be an extensive inclusive list that is representative of a leader's role in the organization. Several examples will now be presented that summarize and further discuss the need for a call to action.

- Within your team you find that the responsibilities are not evenly distributed, despite your appeals from the team to contribute more frequently and with greater effort made to your project, program, or portfolio.
- You are working with a specialist who doesn't always take your suggestions into consideration when needed, and it is negatively affecting your desired outcomes on your project, program, or portfolio.
- Your manager is frequently dealing with a "crisis," and you are not getting the time you need from this person when you need it; as a result your project, program, or portfolio is suffering the consequences.
- You require the cooperation and commitment of someone from another department or organization for your project, program, or portfolio.

These examples provided just some of the challenges that a project, program, or portfolio manager may occur while working in a matrix structure. Each challenge was addressed in this book across the chapters. It is important as a takeaway to recognize and agree with these statements. They are the common barriers that are faced by someone in your role in a matrix structure. A team member may also face these challenges, and it is your responsibility to ensure completion of work has been made. When work is completed, there are varied levels of ways it can be brought into the organization and your project, program, or portfolio. The goal is A–Z coverage and inclusion into your tasks. This is done by addressing the needs to influence and convey importance in your message to others. You convey importance by making key players aware of what they need to do and having an action plan to implement your tasks and goals. Over communicating is one way to battle communication challenges that will be faced. Over communicate to those involved in writing and verbally. This is also true when there are greater needs for complexity and accuracy of doing something for the first time. If you accomplish what is in this small list you are well on your way to being successful in your organization. Dealing with a manager who is always in a crisis and not getting the time you and your project, program, or portfolio deserves greatly limits your overall effectiveness and your teams work in a matrix structure.

It is worthy to mention that your team in most instances is actually more important than yourself when viewed by list of overall accomplishments. Your team is the collection of individuals who carry out the orders of your project, program, and portfolio. They make decisions daily on a different level that effect the overall mission and goal that you created on the onset of the project, program, or within your portfolio. Having the team's mission, values, and goals truly helps align your team so everyone has an understanding of the purpose of the work to be done and their specific responsibilities will cause fewer communication gaps and rework in your project or program. Sometimes, the game of "telephone" happens in your work where one person tells another how they interpreted a situation. Always aim to have no more than two levels of communication when conveying important messages and try to keep it from the source when possible. Perhaps, designate one person for internal team communication that all information goes through to ensure transparency. Leaving that up to you as the project, program, or portfolio manager can be taxing and a burden to relay messages and mandates from the organization or yourself to your team.

It should go without saying that you are going to require the cooperation of others in other departments and groups perhaps in another organization during the course of your daily work. First, take the time to establish ground rules and open communication rather than jumping into issues to provide a more healthy and symbiotic relationship where all parties' goals and concerns are addressed not in a vacuum but openly and transparently for everyone to see and contribute to as the work is done.

This approach can be quite true when working with a "specialist," which is very common for this type of organizational designs. Specialists themselves are a specific breed of individuals who required subject matter expertise. They may have a narrow focus about the overall work, but it enables them to remain on target for their job but can run into issues when you want them to see the "big picture" or cooperate outside of their area of expertise on occasion. Their concerns are genuine and are often how to preserve their area they work in and not dilute or take away from it by adding in other areas of work or duties for themselves. They are a master at their specialty and want to avoid or simplify outside interference by others as much as possible. Recognizing their specific focus will help when dealing with these types of subject matter experts as their strengths lie in their need to provide critical information to the required work. By doing so, these experts can continuously make meaningful contributions to the organization and your project, program, or portfolio work.

One way in eventually distributing responsibilities is to write them down, categorize them, and assign priorities among your team. It is important that this list be error free, easy to read, and understand. There can be no worse crime than creating a list to assign tasks if it is unclear and lacks the basics from which to make decisions. If any document does not serve its intended use, remove it while you get feedback from those who work with it and improve it. Having artifacts from previous project, program, or portfolio managers in your work can create confusion if they were not effective.

Chapter 3 looked at your organization structure. It goes without saying that not being able to fully understand your organizational structure will limit your effectiveness and efficiency in your work. That chapter discussed areas as horizontal relationships, the six bases of power, managing relationships and how to work within a power struggle or with gatekeepers. These are all common in the matrix structure regardless of the industry where you work, the size of your project, program, or portfolio or number of people within your organization. It is critical to understand this chapter for a better focus on ways to make clear and thoughtful decisions. In simple terms, when you grasp the concepts of your organizational design, history, key players, how to interface with varied management groups or individuals you will right away improve your projects, programs, and work in your portfolio. One of the most common way, which is somewhat effective just not efficient, is learning by working for the organization for a long period of time. Over time you will be able to fill in the blanks, but we do not want you waiting years to manage your work as successfully as you can. Forming partnerships with key players and employees who have been with the organization for a longer period of time can provide the valuable gaps that you have of the history and how "things get done here." Chapter 3 looked at many areas that can be brought up for discussion and is not an end-all point but is a good base for you to work from and customize depending on your specific situation and needs.

We are now going to examine and summarize key points of the survey that was done of the 55 project, program, and portfolio managers that was used as a starting point for this book. The majority of survey members had between 4–9 years of experience with a notable amount having between 14 and 20+ years of experience as a project, program, or portfolio manager. What this tells you is that people in only one group did not dominate the survey, and this book has been written for people who are at different levels of their career but all work in a matrix structure. They all require different informational needs and have specific priorities. A project manager with 4 years of experience needs guidance on more foundational topics while a senior program manager with 15 years of solid experience requires a higher level strategic point of view. This book tended not to focus on the numbers of years of experience but what anyone at any level would need to manage in a matrix structure. Some topics were more geared for someone relatively new to this structure, while others such as organizational currency existed for more advanced users. When a book is developed in this manner reflecting back on how you did something in the past and does it need to be addressed comes up, its goal is to break bad habits that may have been formed earlier on or to show others the correct way to avoid them in the future. Breaking habits old or new is not easy and requires constant attention and diligence to make a moderate level of change. Most people shy away from change and settle for what they are comfortable with doing. This is where bad habits are formed. They may not have had a manager in the past who sought to change this habit or was unsuccessful in a previous attempt.

Chapter 4 is something that a lot of people have good intentions to do but lack greater details on the subject. The benefit of volunteering is not just the work itself, but more can be gained if one is strategic and has game plan prior to applying for a volunteer position. There is much that can be captured by the individual. Using it in training groups to improve a skill such as public speaking, coaching others, or being a leader onto itself are compelling reasons to venture in a volunteer role. Time commitments for the most part are minimal and accommodating to your schedule. These organizations would not exist if they were rigid with their volunteers. What is key is to make a plan prior to looking for a volunteer role. Understand what you are trying to accomplish and list ways that you feel a volunteer role can contribute to your goals. Narrow down the list and concentrate on three to five areas that you are looking for your volunteer role. Never forget time commitment. Some roles require a minimum of one year, while others require just a day for an event as an example. Choosing a volunteer organization gives you the opportunity to network; so in addition to improving your skills you are addressing your future career goals! Volunteering can also serve as a place to go when your work is chaotic, and you need a break. You can be mindful of your new surroundings and leave any work-related challenges at bay. This "break" can help see the big picture and give you the needed space to regroup for your regular day job.

There was an astounding 52 to 53 respondents from the survey who felt that the ability to influence team members and outsiders contributed to the success of their role in a matrix structure. This solidifies what this book is trying to teach. You *must* be able to influence the people you work with such as your stakeholders, team members, management, administration staff, customers, and the list goes on. In a matrix structure you *cannot* be successful to any degree without the use of influence. The sooner you hone in on your inner skills to grow this needed skillset, the sooner you will lower the stress and need to count on others to back you up for the work you are trying to accomplish at the moment. It is no wonder why a high majority of survey respondents felt they were overall successful in their role and they attribute their influencing skills as a key ingredient toward success. Advanced technical skills or computer skills does little to gain influence in the organization. Even for a technology company, people skills reign for senior leaders who have to communicate the corporate vision or manage projects, programs, and portfolios.

It should be noted that there were a number of preparation methods used by leaders for matrix structures while consulting with a peer got highest responses, reading a book or online research tied for second. The most shocking number was only 2 of the 51 responses spoke to their human resources department about preparing for their role. This has been a trend over the past several decades to transfer the responsibly to the learner versus another person or group within the company. With highly specialized jobs it is just more efficient to leave it to the individual to select the ways he or she will learn new information. There always has to be management support and allocating time and resources for such learning of course. Mapping out a 5- and 10-year plan that you share with your manager is one of the ways you can gain support for your efforts and feedback on areas that you may not have thought about previously. When you discuss career planning with your manager you will often find there are different avenues that you can take. Reflecting and trying to meet the most of your requirements can be challenging and stretch positions that take you from one level up to the next are bound to be in your favor. The full survey results can be seen in the appendix of this book for those wishing to take a deeper dive at the numbers. Studying the data collected can benefit you in understanding where your corporation fits in the results and what is best suited for you in your career.

The survey demonstrated that there is still improvement needed by project, program, and portfolio managers who have even more than 20 years of experience in this area. Utilizing Massive Open Online Courses (MOOCs) from top universities is one new method of acquiring knowledge at your own pace. With no cost to you other than your time MOOCs are just another tool that you should be utilizing. These short online courses teach you the essentials of a topic in a format that provides some feedback in terms of a quiz or course completion assignment. Online education has been going through much evolution in the past 10 years and is a major player for adult education options. The notion of driving to a course after work makes it unreasonable for some, and these options now provide the working capacity to learn a new skill or of subject for their job as a project, program, or portfolio manager. You will be quickly surprised as to the organization and modern learning that they can provide. The reason postsecondary education is discussed in a topic of operating in a matrix structure is twofold: to acquire a new skill and to stay current in your existing skillset. Online education does not mean sitting in a room alone with no one to answer your questions. You have your peer group or instructor that you can reach out to at any time and as well it increases your network. Blended learning, which is a mix of online and on campus, is also a solution where you want some face time with peers and your instructor. The configuration options for taking a course are endless and should not be the reason not to pursue any course. It is your duty to be resourceful and ask the right questions to make meaningful contributions.

8.1 What Are the Next Steps?

The final section of this conclusion is going to discuss exactly how you should proceed with your new found wealth of information from this book. Practical lists have been made for your first 90 days on the job in a matrix structure now that you have read this book. There are discussions that have to take place between key individuals and your team members. Action plans have to be made and adapted to any project, program, or portfolio manager role.

8.1.1 90-Day Action Plan

1. Identify key stakeholders, trusted employees, and those who act as the hub of information within the company.

2. Build relationships that benefit all parties. Reach across the aisle to mend any poor experiences that person may have had in the past dealing with someone in your role.

3. Sit with your manager and identify what priorities you should be trying to achieve within your first 90 days. Your list and your manager's may differ slightly.

4. Meet with every one of your customers internally or externally and set a clear path for communication going forward.

5. Do you research? What worked in the past? What was tried and what was not tried as of yet? Do not let this list take over your future goals but use it to serve as a warning, not a direction, that you should heed.

6. Identify a volunteer role that helps you gain influence or build a skill that is needed in the role.

These six actionable items *must* be done, but the order is left up to you depending on your unique situation and goals that you are trying to achieve. Always remember that preparation upfront means greater success and less challenges when there is a plan in place. A plan is a detailed proposal of what one is to do. The more required, the more detail is asked of you. It is rare that your situation does not need a plan in place. Simply writing down what is in your head gains you an advantage. Ninety days have been chosen as three months is enough time to get comfortable in the role and company. You have gotten to meet all those who you will be involved with and given opportunity to challenge yourself and lead others. As a project, program, or portfolio manager you may be taking over for someone else, and work in process is always harder to learn than beginning from the start. If that does not suggest why an action plan has to be made then little else can be made as a case.

These discussions outlined below are not seven single discussions. Rather, they are seven separate discussion strategies that happen throughout your first 90 days and some beyond. As with the 90-day action plan there is no formal process for these, but they all are recommended at some point during the first 90 days of your taking on the role of project, program, or portfolio manager in a matrix structure. There may be, in fact, more items that must happen for you in your first 90 days. Do not use these lists as an all-inclusive but as a good baseline that you are to customize and expand accordingly. It would be advisable to share your first 90 days lists with your manager to gain feedback and buy-in.

8.1.2 Discussions to Take Place within the First 90 Days

1. Determine and create a stakeholder matrix.
2. Meet with all customers (internal and external).
3. Discuss communication strategies with your team.
4. Meet with your manager to outline high-level strategies that you are to achieve.
5. Identify any gaps within your project, program, or portfolio. Build trust that you will correct these gaps and follow through with your intentions.
6. Look for quick wins in all areas of your job function. Set aside long strategic plans for after your first 90 days.
7. Form a coalition for the purpose of achieving your strategy. Perhaps you want to reduce development time or increase customer retention.

Your manager most likely has formed relationships with your customers, team members, and others in your organization. Fully utilize your manager to your benefit. Do not shy away from your goals and intentions. You will be surprised to see what support will come your way in your short 90-day journey. You will make a name for yourself as one who takes initiative and is an expert in his or her field. This will help in your efforts to build or expand a coalition in your organization.

Although this book provided information and new knowledge it equally opened areas that can be earmarked for improvement and many questions that can now be asked. It provided enough relevant information to make a difference in your position whether you are new to the role or have been in it for 10 years. The base of this book came from my dissertation where I sought to reduce employee turnover and increase workplace commitment. It must come as no surprise as the structure of this book and the chapter headings that were made. You are looking to increase your commitment in your role and reduce the various reasons that can cause employee turnover. The saying knowledge is power is far too accurate and hard to miss for this book. What is required is your commitment to improve your skillset (communication, influence, organizational knowledge, leadership, etc.) and not rely on your technical background in your field. Far too often those in project, program, or portfolio management roles were promoted for their technical skills and ability to get things done. What was not emphasized in all cases was being a self-made leader.

Appendix

The following is the complete survey answers in its entirety that formulated the direction of this book.

Survey Question 1:
How many years of experience do you have as a project, program, or portfolio manager? See Figure A.1 for the results.

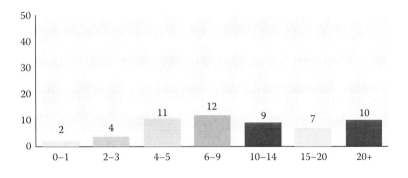

Figure A.1 Participants' years of experience.

Survey Question 2:
Has volunteer roles within your organization (committees, groups, etc.) inside or outside the organization in professional groups (such as PMI)

increased your influence and ability in your role inside the organization? See Figure A.2 for results.

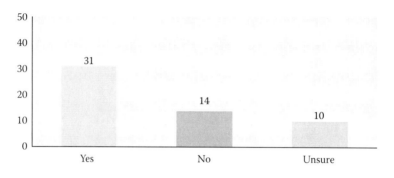

Figure A.2   Effect of volunteering.

Survey Question 3:
Do you feel that your ability to influence team members, outsiders, and other leaders inside and outside the organization contribute to the success of your role? See Figure A.3 for results.

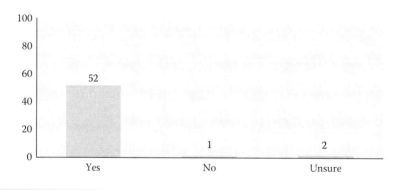

Figure A.3   Effect of influence on success.

Survey Question 4:
Did you feel you were overall successful in the role of project, program, or portfolio manager without formal authority over your team? See Figure A.4 for results.

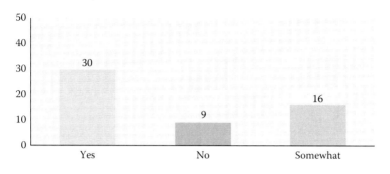

Figure A.4 Perception of success.

Survey Question 5:

What did you do to prepare yourself for your project, program, or portfolio management role in a matrix environment? See Figure A.5 for results.

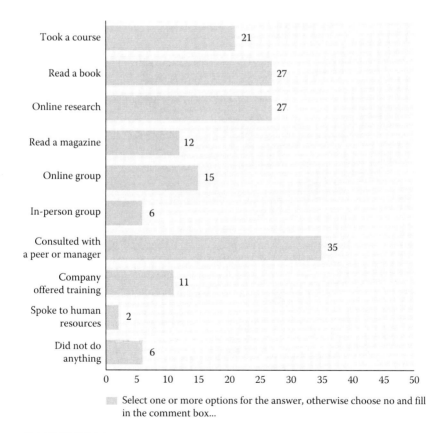

Select one or more options for the answer, otherwise choose no and fill in the comment box...

Figure A.5 Types of preparation.

Survey Question 6:

What communication method did you find most useful when conveying important information to your team members that you do not have formal authority over? See Figure A.6 for results.

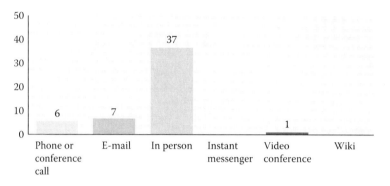

Figure A.6 Communication methods.

Survey Question 7:

Specifically, what do you do in order to get cooperation from a team member who you did not have authority over?

NUMBER	RESPONSE
1	Explain the importance of the task he or she is doing for the team and himself or herself.
2	Explain why a course of action matters to them/the project.
3	Enticing.
4	Give my opinion, ask for their views, and support for their success.
5	I try to find some common ground, build a relationship, and then outline the benefits and opportunities for the team member. The WIFM factor.
6	Meetings require input into WBS development and schedule, clearly delineate responsibilities. Work with resource managers to ensure resource assignments.
7	Agreed for a Goal/Action to be executed by team member as part of roles and responsibility in matrix organization, which is must to meet business/customer requirement.
8	Approach person or person's manager trying to get approval and push cooperation. Proposed to participation in person's evaluation report.
9	Empathy that you understand their concerns and display that you can remove obstacles that come in their way during delivery. Instill confidence in team members, that the manager is unbiased and has good ethics.
10	I work with their manager first to obtain their approval to have that team member work with me. The manager usually will assign someone who has experience in the field that I am looking for.

(Continued)

NUMBER	RESPONSE
11	Use a velvet hammer and persuasion.
12	Connect with the team regularly.
13	Involve team member's manager through regular updates and status meetings.
14	Talk to them.
15	I used one-on-one discussions to communicate the project situation and what it was that I needed cooperation from. This enabled me and the person(s) to empathize the problem and environment much better than otherwise possible through other forms of communication, that is, e-mail, memo, etc.
16	Explain the importance of what we are doing.
17	Group meetings, memos.
18	Had meetings with such team members and made them understand the importance of the program and their contribution toward it.
19	Try to present the natural barriers to implementing the project, i.e., cultural differences in foreign markets for successfully changing business strategies.
20	Relationship building was the most critical. I earned their respect by not being a subject matter expert but rather by providing them with organization, main point of contact, and follow up. After gaining the respect of the team members, it was much easier to gain cooperation from all parties.
21	Agree about the how and when with the line manager; also have periodic reviews and contact with the line manager.
22	Keep focus on program value and benefits for organization.
23	1. Physical presence often to stay at the top of mind. 2. Make relation between project (or program) objectives and the individual's key job and personal benefits for engaging in the project. 3. Reference the authority (manager or otherwise) that has assigned the person to be part of the project.
24	Provide incentives.
25	Ask for their support, in person.
26	Establish and maintain professional relationships. Also use common personal interests to build trust and mutual respect.
27	Build personal relationships with others.
28	Formal request for resources.
29	Develop the culture of harmony and cooperation with reminder of ultimate benefits that program will deliver.
30	Share the benefits for the organization and the opportunity for learning.
31	Personal conversation.
32	Servant leadership style.

(Continued)

NUMBER	RESPONSE
33	In order to get cooperation from a team member I always try to explain the logic behind a request or a task. It frequently triggers a discussion about a proposed approach, related program issues and risks, etc. I find it stimulating and helpful for both parties to understand a particular issue or a task better. Even if I cannot convince a team member that a proposed approach is the best option for the given situation, it still helps to get a buy-in from the team member because he understands where I am coming from.
34	Create an atmosphere of open, honest, timely communication.
35	Ensure the project focus was clear, a series of check-ins often, open communication.
36	1. Collect his or her feedback. 2. Get his or her buy-in (as much as possible). 3. Set clear expectation and team goal, including his or hers, in public.
37	Negotiate in person! Show how the results can be beneficial to the person being convinced.
38	One example: Team member was not getting his work done. When asked, he would tell me it was nothing personal, just had too much going on. I went over his head, but was able to get his commitment by framing it as getting him the help he needed…and actually coming through with it.
39	Ask for their ideas and input…empowerment.
40	Took them for coffee.
41	I ensure that I have done my homework and have understood the issue to the extent possible. They appreciate that I understand the work that they do and thereby willing to cooperate more.
42	I hold personal and group conversations about roles and responsibilities from various viewpoints and to determine the best means of communication. My method is listening and guiding while, at the same time, establishing processes, guidelines, and expectations for interactions and deliverables.
43	I ensure that they know how valuable they are to the project and in general.
44	As I said earlier, matrix organization's culture helps you to have that authority to get the cooperation from team members. If they are not cooperating, you can escalate to functional manager. After all, you are responsible for delivery of the project.
45	Get his or her manager involved. Let him or her feel that he or she belongs to the project/program team.
46	Transparency and sincerity.
47	Play to their stake in the situation and impact. Share the bigger picture and include them in decision making/planning.
48	Peer pressure, shame, and if all else fails appropriate management escalation.
49	I try to explain project benefits and how it could add value to our customers.
50	It has never been a problem.

Survey Question 8:
Which best describes the role of the individual who was most helpful to you in your job? See Figure A.7 for results.

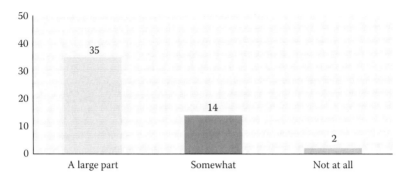

Figure A.7 Positions of the most helpful individual in participants' organizations.

Survey Question 9:
Was organizational culture a factor in a role of leadership without formal authority in the organization? See Figure A.8 for results.

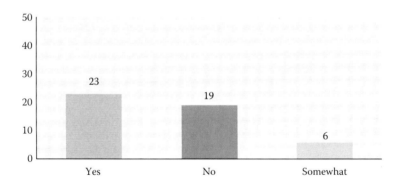

Figure A.8 Role of organizational culture.

Survey Question 10:
What was your biggest barrier to success in your role as a program manager in a matrix environment?

NUMBER	RESPONSE
1	Not yielding, able to answer the need of a higher salary from team members who performed well.
2	Clarifying role of a project manager on a core team.
3	Communication.
4	Getting buy-in from project managers especially when you are sometimes thought of as redundant when formal authority is not bestowed. I had to extend trust before I could get theirs.
5	Selection of team members.
6	No authority, resources being reassigned to work that their manager feels is more important (there have to be organizational priorities set so this doesn't happen).
7	Getting functional managers understanding the importance of project management and extending support from respective team.
8	Senior manager's cooperation as they were overloaded from other duties. This caused delays to some parts of the project.
9	Team members having different functional managers within the same team that I handled.
10	The lack of understanding what a program manager is and how to best leverage a program manager. The misconception is that most companies believe that a program manager is a very senior project manager who can Manage Multiple Complex Projects at the same time.
11	Lack of specific detailed knowledge of a product or hidden process.
12	Executive support and relaying program importance.
13	Unclear lines of authority/direction at different levels.
14	Lack of ability to immediately engage the needed resource whenever "I" needed that person w/o first discussing the need from that resources functional manager.
15	The functional manager.
16	The lack of formal authority.
17	Functional managers.
18	Safety and human resources.
19	Predetermined direction by others without due consideration for the business environment.
20	In my example, it was a clinical EMR implementation executed by the "IT" department. Our biggest barrier continues to be having IT PMO as primary proficient project/program management executors over the entire implementation, but still viewed as "IT" rather than just program management for the program no matter what the content. This is an example of an organizational/cultural transformation that must also be the scope of the program manager, not just ensuring the system is implemented successfully. This has been a huge cultural obstacle. Often can be a felt as a "stay out of my business—you are just IT" from other departments.
21	Priority setting by line management.

(*Continued*)

NUMBER	RESPONSE
22	Forced external decisions by senior leadership instead of relying to program manager and his or her team judgment.
23	1. Conflicting priorities for the person's time. 2. Time (long running projects tend to become less of *a priority* of time).
24	Lack of authority on the team and communications.
25	Finding accurate data inputs.
26	Lack of full control on program team members. Conflicting priorities.
27	Making sure that subject matter experts do not lose track of schedule. Individual department policies not aligned with program was the biggest barrier.
28	Confusion with processes.
29	The changes in the PM processes for the executive team.
30	Sometime cross orders and focus need.
31	Lack of clear definition of roles and responsibilities.
32	Program executive sponsor. We not always saw a program execution strategy eye to eye and it made my work much harder. While I had a lot of support from my manager, it helped just marginally since executive sponsor was higher in a company's hierarchy.
33	Management not providing a clear prioritization of competing resources.
34	Not sure.
35	People, people's conflict of interests, people's hidden agendas.
36	Organizational culture.
37	Being "the new guy" in such an environment. It takes more time to earn the respect and trust of people who do not report to you.
38	Multinational work force and cultural ideologies.
39	The inertia of against change in large organizations.
40	Uncertainty regarding the time the team members can actually put in as against their willingness/interest to complete the task.
41	Establishing commitment from individuals in the face of conflicting demands from other managers.
42	Ladder climbing, self-centered swine.
43	Since resources are shared, getting the priority to your project is the biggest challenge. It depends on how you negotiate for this.
44	Coordination—straightforward communication—collaboration from individuals' managers.
45	Disruptions from day to day, nonproject, operational tasks.
46	Formal authority, number of organizational silos, teams/organization goal alignment. Team's workloads are over allocated.
47	The warranty of resource schedule, because they change their priority (or allocation) as their manager needs.
48	None.

Survey Question 11:

Specifically, did a past role in the organization prepare you for being in a leadership role without authority? See Figure A.9 for results.

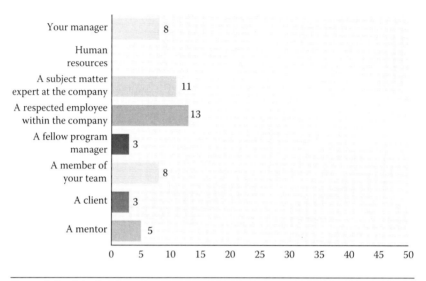

Figure A.9 Role of past experience.

Survey Question 12:

Did you feel others perceived you in a certain way in your role without formal authority from the onset? Choose one of the following that best describes your situation. See Figure A.10 for results.

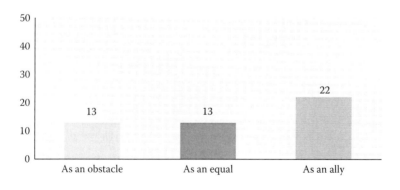

Figure A.10 Perception of participants by others in their organizations.

Survey Question 13:

State any other factors that have provided positive impact for success in your role in the organization, which you did not have authority in. In other words, your secret sauce for program management in a matrix environment.

NUMBER	RESPONSE
1	To listen to people and try to help them.
2	Establish competency and trust early on.
3	Good communication and sympathy (entice).
4	First extend trust before getting their trust. Be patient as every project is unique and every project manager is humanly unique.
5	First, senior leadership support for project management and resource allocation. Second, organizational priorities set for projects and projects vs. maintenance work or other tasks. Third, clear delineation of roles and responsibilities.
6	Team management, splitting and delegating customer requirements to team members, project reviews/status updates.
7	Appreciation by senior management and fellow managers, good relations and communication with people who have power inside the organization.
8	Bring in established processes and ask the team to adhere to it.
	Be transparent and neutral.
	Own the program and defend the team members in front of other teams, but tell the team members way to improve or eliminate past mistakes in person.
	Give constant feedback about resources to the functional managers.
9	Obtaining a lot of education on learning how to implement program management. I would then take that information and create processes and policies that would allow the company to successfully leverage program management.
10	1. Educate the functional managers on how to work in a matrix environment. Both functional managers and program managers must be able to strike a balance on how both can succeed in a company w/o the detriment of the other.
	2. Use examples of where programs were successful and what roles the function managers played. Balance this with failures and let downs as well.
	3. Make sure that upper management has an awareness of the complexity of matrix environments in your particular program, and that the program sponsor will actively participate in assuring resources are readily available.
	4. Consider evaluating functional and program/project managers as a "pool" in lieu of individuals. This will motivate both parties to provide mutual cooperation as well as enable both to meet corporate goals and objectives.
	5. Determine the "type" of matrix organization the company is using, that is, weak, strong, and composite. Based on this, the company should revise job descriptions to support this structure through enhanced job design and accountability going forward.
	6. Work very hard at soft skills. Resource sharing in most companies creates a great amount of conflict within, thus the program manager needs to have very strong negotiation and people skills to better manage the program while keeping the resource pool motivated and left in-tact after program completion.

(Continued)

NUMBER	RESPONSE
11	Team work, good team spirit, group support for all members, gratitude to all involved in case of success, remarkable own work input in any project.
12	Communication and resource management.
13	For program management.
14	Communication and educating of external team members of complexes of doing business in foreign country.
15	Secret sauce is communication, relationship building, and stakeholder management.
16	Define shared (line and program) objectives and benefits with the team member and his boss.
17	Learn thinking and enablers for program management.
18	Expert knowledge in the domain.
19	I already had great relationships. I fostered those relationships by always including these folks in decision-making processes.
20	Good relations. Genuine empathy toward others. Patience.
21	Making sure that everyone feels that their role is important for the ultimate benefits being delivered.
22	Clearly scheduled task list with managed dependencies.
23	Nonauthoritative management style.
24	In regard to question #12. Some individual contributors perceived me as an obstacle. Customers perceived me as an ally because I was pushing for results which customers have expected—not what the company was preferring to do in order to cut corners. At the end, I was able to prove that the approach I took was a better way in a long term and it contributed to my ability to lead other people without formal authority.
25	It is all about creating and maintaining good relationships with your team. Since you do not have formal authority, you want them to *want* to work on your team. Show interest in their personal and professional goals; give them credit for their contributions as often and as loudly as possible.
26	Asking for input/advice, listening, listening and listening. Empowering all as equals.
27	Learn as much as possible about the work other team members do. They are willing to go the extra mile when they understand you know the content and effort required for the tasks.
28	Frequent personal and group communication with people who are or may be affected by the program.
29	Most of my resources view me as an ally or mentor.
30	My flexibility to approach anybody for getting things done. Communication at all levels helps program managers.
31	To respect the team and their limitations due to the matrix environment.

References

A Guide to the Project Management Body of Knowledge (PMBOK guide) (5th edn.). 2013. Newtown Square, PA: Project Management Institute, p. 22.

Broverman, I. K., Vogel, S. R., Broverman, D. M., Clarkson, F. E., and Rosenkrantz, P. S. 1972. Sex role stereotypes: A current appraisal. *Journal of Social Issues*, *28*(2), 59–78.

Cohen, A. R. and Bradford, D. L. 2005. *Influence without Authority*. Hoboken, NJ: Wiley.

Dupont, C. 1996. Negotiation as coalition building. Journal International negotiation (Hague, Netherlands). *Journal Citation Reports*, *1*(1), 60–61.

Falbo, T. and Peplau, L. A. 1980. Power strategies in intimate relationships. *Journal of Personality and Social Psychology*, *38*, 618–628.

Gouldner, A. W. 1960. The norm of reciprocity: A preliminary statement. *American Sociological Review*, *35*, 161–178.

Grant, R. 2005. *Contemporary Strategy Analysis* (5th edn.). Malden, MA: Blackwell Publishing, p. 7, 245.

Johnson, P. 1976. Women and power: Toward a theory of effectiveness. *Journal of Social Issues*, *32*(3), 99–110.

Raven, B. H. 1993. The bases of power: Origins and recent developments. *Journal of Social Issues*, *49*, 227–251.

Raven, B. H. and Kruglanski, A. W. 1970. Conflict and power. In P. Swingle (Ed.), *The Structure of Conflict* (pp. 69–109). New York: Academic Press.

Stein, L. I. 1971. Male and female: The doctor-nurse game. In J. P. Spradley and D. W. McCurdy (Eds.), *Conformity and Conflict: Readings in Cultural Anthropology* (pp. 185–193). Boston: Little, Brown.

Walster, E., Walster, G. W., and Berscheid, E. 1978. *Equity Theory and Research*. Boston: Allyn & Bacon.

Index